There is no more critical period in human intellectual development than the first twenty-four months of life.

"The ability to be critical, to verify, to be prepared to reject the first idea that is presented if necessary—this is what we must instill in our children, and indeed in our society as a whole."

From Dr. S.H. Jacob's *Your Baby's Mind*

The subject of this book—the dawning of intellect—has far-reaching implications not only for parents, but also for educators, childcare professionals, and all with an interest in the world our children will both shape and inherit when they reach adulthood.

How do babies learn from birth through age two? And how can we help them develop their fullest intellectual potential, enabling them to grow into healthy and confident young people?

DR. S. H. JACOB

YOUR BABY'S MIND

DR. S. H. JACOB

YOUR BABY'S MIND

BOB ADAMS, INC.
PUBLISHERS
Holbrook, Massachusetts

ISBN: 1-55850-137-1

Published by Bob Adams, Inc.
260 Center Street
Holbrook, Massachusetts, 02343

Printed in the United States of America

J I H G F E D C B A

This publication is designed to provide accurate information with regard to the subject matter covered. It is not, and is not intended to be, a substitute for consultation with a qualified physician or therapist. If medical advice or other expert assistance is required, the services of a competent professional in the field should be sought.

The tables on pages 215-219 are reproduced from Linda Smolak's *Infancy*, ©1986, p. 238. Reprinted by permission of Prentice Hall, Englewood Cliffs, New Jersey.

Cover photo © Photo Researchers, Inc.
Cover design by Joyce C. Weston

*To my daughter Beth Ann,
who filled my heart with joy
as an infant and who continues
to do so in young adulthood.*

CONTENTS

ACKNOWLEDGMENTS

The enterprise of writing a book is not accomplished without the cooperative assistance of many people. This book is no exception. It pleases me greatly to acknowledge and thank the individuals who helped me actualize this project.

My first debt, of course, is to my daughter, Beth Ann, who, as an infant, helped me to translate my knowledge of Piaget's theories and observations into a wonderful personal reality. (Many of my observations of her infant behavior are related in this book.) As a young university student, she contributed directly to this book by assembling many of the games and activities found in the Appendices.

I wish to thank Candice Fuhrman, who recognized the potential of this work; Bob Adams, who showed such faith in it; Brandon Toropov, who arduously and skillfully edited the manuscript; Katherine Layzer, Elizabeth Gale, and Robin Hayden for their invaluable assistance in the early stages of this project; Anna Botelho for her excellent work on the book's physical format; Joyce Weston, who designed the striking cover; and Meryl Brenner, who created the illustrations.

Finally, I would like to express my gratitude to my students, who helped me sharpen my knowledge of Piaget's enormous contributions.

BEFORE YOU BEGIN...

THIS IS NOT A PROGRAM designed to raise geniuses. I would not argue that parents could—or should—attempt to do that. I do feel that what *is* needed today, however, is an appreciation of how important it is to pay attention to our infants' and our young children's intellectual growth, and an acknowledgment of the crucial nature of the development that occurs in the first twenty-four months of life.

While *Your Baby's Mind* is written for parents, its subject—the dawning of intellect—has far-reaching implications that may interest others as well, particularly educators and child care professionals. Surely, with our burgeoning nationwide problems in the areas of illiteracy, school performance, and falling levels of international competitiveness, the issue of how the minds of our children grow is a fundamental one.

The questions this book sets out to answer are immensely important: How do babies learn from birth through age two? And how can we as parents help them develop their fullest intellectual potential, enabling them to grow into healthy and confident young people? *Your Baby's Mind* is about involvement in nurturing your baby's

- intelligence,
- curiosity,
- inventiveness,
- sense of discovery,
- desire to explore,
- judgment,
- reasoning,
- humor,
- and general adaptability to the environment.

Babies and children develop in discrete, well-known stages. Knowing what those stages are, you can enhance and enrich your baby's life by playing games that excite her *because* of the way she is currently developing.

This is a vitally important process. Neglecting cognitive development can lead to frustration, boredom, and perhaps even an incomplete preparation for later childhood. By the same token, pushing a child ahead of her own development runs the risk of leaving her frustrated, overstressed, and convinced that most of her efforts will yield only a sense of failure.

The majority of parents, given the opportunity, are very eager to learn to observe and understand their baby's activities as expressions of intelligence. To make it easier to translate the abstractions of developmental stages into the specific accomplishments of a baby—*your* baby—we will also look at a variety of interesting and stage-appropriate toys, games, and activities designed especially to enrich your baby's experiences.

While these activities with your baby are certainly enjoyable, they also yield immeasurable long-range beneficial results. Understanding *why* what you are doing is important will enable you to expand on the suggestions contained here, creating your own repertoire of enriching experiences.

Your baby's mind is perhaps the most miraculous thing you will ever encounter—and the more you know, the more miraculous the encounter will become!

Dr. S.H. Jacob
Santa Monica, California

◆

CHAPTER ONE

How Do Babies Learn?

CHILDREN FORM KNOWLEDGE BY ACTING upon the objects or the ideas they are trying to understand.

Babies are born with a number of reflex actions, such as grasping, sucking, and swallowing, as well as various eye movements, such as blinking, focusing, and tracking. These are the only means by which newborns experience the world around them. These reflex actions, which constitute their means of survival, form the basis for early mental development.

» When Beth grasps a rough object, like a carrot, she learns to differentiate it from a smooth one, like a banana. Even though these actions are restricted to a few movements and a few primitive perceptions, Beth comes equipped to act. Within a month or so, she learns to coordinate these reflex actions with one another, thereby expanding her knowledge and extending the ways in which she gains additional knowledge, as when she hears and follows your fingers as you snap them in front of her in a side-to-side movement.

« When David learns to integrate seeing his rattle with a grasping motion, he can reach for it and grab it. As he coordinates grasping with sucking, he can bring the rattle to his mouth.

It is through coordinations of reflexes that babies grow in intelligence.

Intelligence springs from actions; the means by which intelligence grows is the coordination of actions.

Such coordinations result in new learning and new and more sophisticated *ways* of knowing.

Babies are active beings. For them to know, they must act. To know is not to be passive; it is not to be drilled, for instance, with written words and pictures of what they represent. Babies are not empty receptacles waiting to be filled with information.

« Babies want—and indeed need—to be active.

« Babies are born with a strong desire to know.

« Babies inherently seek stimulation.

» Babies love to explore and manipulate.

» Babies enjoy trying out newly acquired skills.

» Babies construct knowledge by acting on—and interacting with—objects around them.

Children are born with a burning desire to make sense of their abilities and their circumstances. Parents and teachers are charged with the fascinating, fulfilling, and rewarding responsibilty of educating and nurturing these inherently human abilities.

PARENTING AND THE PIAGET ALTERNATIVE

What Sigmund Freud is to personality theory, and what Albert Einstein is to theoretical physics, Jean Piaget is to child development and genetic epistemology. (We define "epistemology" as the study of the nature, basis, limits, and validity of human knowledge.) Piaget's contributions to the fields of child psychology, educational psychology, and cognitive development are enormous. His classic observations on the development of intelligence in children, as well as the theories arising from them, are widely studied today.

Although he showed signs of genius early in life, earning a Ph.D. in natural sciences by the age of twenty-one, Piaget's interest in psychology did not really emerge until 1921, when he was twenty-five. At this point, he became keenly interested in biology's relevance to issues of knowledge and turned his attention to the work of

Alfred Binet, a Frenchman famous for his work in developing the famous intelligence quotient ("I.Q.") test.

Binet focused on the correct answers to the mental puzzles he had created; Piaget was most interested in the *errors* made by children who took the test. He noticed certain distinct patterns of wrong answers among children of roughly the same age group. These patterns were of great interest to him, and, in turn, to all who followed in the field of cognitive development. After all, if a pattern is attributable to age, and if no one ever deliberately *teaches* a wrong answer, then the responses must be linked somehow to the *way* intellect develops.

Let's assume that we ask a number of children, "Which weighs more, a pound of feathers or a pound of clay?" If most (or perhaps all) the children respond, "A pound of clay," then what is at issue is not how much has been learned, but the way knowing itself is made possible—specifically, the child's ability to grasp the concept of a pound of something being equivalent to a pound of anything else.

Through such analysis of incorrect answers, Piaget came to believe that the measurement of intelligence (otherwise known as "psychometrics") may be useful for determining what children have *learned*, but not for discovering how children *think*. His subsequent work at the University of Geneva emphasized clinical observations of children and infants responding to intellectual challenge.

Piaget's work yielded the most comprehensive examination to date of intellectual development in the young. This trailblazing work was by no means a series of dry abstractions: his descriptions and theories began with his observations of his own three children, Jacqueline, Lucienne, and Laurent. Piaget's landmark 1936 work, *The Origins of Intelligence in Children*, still stands as a milestone in the study of infant intelligence.

OPPORTUNITIES FOR GROWTH

Piaget's views on education stress intellectual development over specific learning "tricks"—learning how to learn, how to think, and not merely learning specific responses to certain cues. It follows that parents can—and should—provide opportunities for their babies to exercise their inborn, natural abilities so that they can grow to be problem-solvers, not rote learners; explorers, not mindless followers; inventors, not copiers.

To provide children with this support from the early days of infancy onward is in keeping with Piaget's most fundamental principles. The methods we will examine in this book contain all the elements of a return to sound, tested child-rearing concepts arranged to work in complete harmony with comfortable, purposeful parenting. My method involves nurturing and educating our children's *underlying processes* of intelligence. This is not the same as "teaching" our infants and children remarkable things so that they will be "advanced." The question is not how to generate performance at a level we as adults might define, but how to make the most of the stage the child is presently in.

 Intelligence does *not* come about by teaching word association with objects, or force-feeding ready-made facts so they may be stored and retrieved on cue.

Such an approach confuses an adult's acquired symbolic learning methods with the more intricate—and far more interesting—developmental processes of a new human mind.

Our goal, then, should be to promote an attitude that permits babies and young children to be active, to discover through their spontaneous actions, and to invent as necessary. It is in this way that parents are of greatest help in promoting intellectual development.

This goal can be accomplished by matching a baby's stage of mental development with appropriately chosen toys, materials, or activities. Without this proper match, baby's abilities could be overestimated or underestimated, and meaningful interactions would be less likely to take place. Equally important, our efforts must always respect and conform to the natural, spontaneous way children form knowledge.

THREE BASIC PRINCIPLES

But how can simple reflex actions—which are, after all, essentially a set of predetermined instructions—lead to the complex achievement that is human knowledge? How, for instance, does a baby construct more elaborate knowledge of a rattle when the only tools of knowing at his disposal are a few rigid reflex actions?

It may be easiest to answer that question by first looking at how a baby *doesn't* come to know a rattle: by reading the word "rattle" written out on a card placed above the crib, or by repeatedly being shown a picture of a rattle. These figurative ways of learning are not an infant's natural ways of knowing, but an adult's.

First, babies construct knowledge by acting on the object they are trying to know. To know a rattle is to know how heavy it is, how it feels, what kind of noise it makes, how it tastes, and how it smells. To know a rattle is to grasp it, shake it, smell it, mouth it. Second, children expand their knowledge by relating what they are trying to know to what they already know. Nothing is more natural than the instinct to relate the new to the old, the to-be-known with the known. If a baby already knows how to reach, grasp, and mouth objects, then a new object gets known exactly by reaching, grasping and mouthing!

Finally, children appropriate knowledge by using it. Once they have acted upon something and related it to their prior knowledge, they need to use it in order to master it and make it their very own. Practicing what has recently been learned is the child's way of giving some permanence to newly acquired knowledge. Although the reason for this tendency toward repetition may not always be clear to parents, the tendency itself is very familiar indeed.

» If throwing a spoon from the high-chair makes mommy pick it up once, then throwing the spoon again and again will make mommy pick it up again and again. If playing peek-a-boo the first time is fun, it is even more fun the tenth time!

Through these principles, we can see that children's knowledge develops in an orderly manner and by means of three main activities. I call this process C.E.O., which stands for *construct, expand,* and *own.*

 1. CONSTRUCT: Children construct knowledge by acting on the object of knowledge.
2. EXPAND: Children expand their knowledge by relating the object of knowledge to what they already know.
3. OWN: Children come to own knowledge by using it.

This general framework offers a subtle yet immensely important implication. We must create the appropriate, comfortable atmosphere for our babies' learning with a consistently warm, caring attitude. This is because, as it turns out, babies develop their fullest intellectual potential through exploration and play, with great latitude to choose what they are interested in, and in an atmosphere of unconditional love, encouragement, and support.

FOUR FACTORS IN INTELLECTUAL DEVELOPMENT

For decades, cognition specialists have pondered the question of mental development. Thanks largely to Piaget's enormous contributions, we now believe that four major factors explain this intriguing process: maturation, physical experience, social transmission, and equilibration, or self-regulation. Let's look at the parts to understand how the whole takes shape.

MATURATION

Biologically, babies come equipped with certain abilities: they grasp objects; they blink; they suck; they perceive depth; they coo; they show a startle reaction when dropped. These are innate capacities, requiring no training or education. Heredity provides the seeds for these capacities, which develop as the nervous system matures. This unfolding process is referred to as maturation.

Experience and the opportunities to exercise these skills enable the baby to improve upon them, expanding them to their natural limits. There can be little argument against the idea that environment plays a significant role in determining the direction and extent to which inherited capacity will be expressed.

> **The child who is raised in a nurturing, warm human environment is likely to develop inherited capacities to their fullest potential. Children raised in a sterile atmosphere rarely fulfill anticipated growth.**

But the process of each baby's maturation does set some limits on the role played by the environment. If an infant is born brain damaged, for example, no degree of environmental stimulation will alter the child's ultimate growth and development limitations. Maturation, then, is a key element in the growth of intellect, and it works in tandem with experience.

Most authorities believe that while mental growth cannot be forced, it certainly can be nurtured in the proper setting. The question is, how? Our answer lies in providing a broad variety of "stage-appropriate" enriching experiences. Let me emphasize again, however, that if the nurturing experiences offered to children are not appropriate to their level of ability, and if they are not given the opportunity to initiate their own actions and choose their own interests, the experiences will be of no benefit at all. They will be worse than worthless, for they will create endless frustration.

To determine what kinds of varied, stage-appropriate experiences are absolutely necessary to enhance intellectual development, we divide experience into two areas: physical—interaction with any aspect of the physical environment—and social—interaction with people and their culture.

PHYSICAL EXPERIENCE

No—not aerobics or pushups! Physical experience, in the context of intellectual development, refers to a person's interaction with any aspect of the physical environment. A baby pushing a ball, shaking a rattle, pulling a toy, banging on the table, or dropping a spoon to the floor is discovering the physical properties of these objects as well as how objects interact with each other. All such encounters with the physical world constitute physical experience, which is crucial to a child's mental development. In fact, it is through this form of experience that a baby builds scientific as well as logico-mathematical knowledge.

« When baby Allison pounds a plastic drinking glass against a bowl, she discovers some properties of the glass: its shape, its transparency, the noise it makes, its weight, its texture, and so on. She discovers the features of the things that she can touch, see, taste, hear, and smell. Gradually she builds a body of knowledge about concrete things and how they influence one another as they act upon one another. For instance, if another glass is clear, feels a certain way, weighs more than the first one, and falls on a hard surface, it will shatter; the first glass, though, is made of something that is lighter, feels different, and even "tastes" different from the first glass, and it will not shatter if dropped. This is the kind of knowledge Allison constructs for herself while interacting with the physical world. Even if her early generalizations are not entirely accurate, they are nonetheless very important, and they will be refined, tested, and revised as time goes on.

A vital aspect of such interactions involves building knowledge of how to interact with these material objects. When a baby interacts with concrete objects and events around her, she discovers how to relate to these objects and events: how to hold a rattle, how to shake it, how to get it to make a certain noise, how to pick it up and how to release it.

> **By actively manipulating objects, Allison discovers two things: regularities in the environment and the effects of her actions upon it.**

It is very important for your baby to interact with a variety of objects and events during her first two years. That is when an appreciation of the world of science is being set.

I use "science" here in its most basic and profound sense: the word is rooted in the Latin verb *sciere*, "to know." If her "experiments" are encouraged, your baby will not only build herself a scientific base but will also develop an inquisitive attitude toward science in general. This knowledge, and especially the attitude toward learning, will eventually have a great impact when she enters school.

You may be surprised to learn that even your child's logic and mathematical knowledge are constructed from these physical experiences. How can a child form mathematical concepts by playing with physical objects? Isn't learning logic and math something that comes much later, something related to the reading and writing of numbers?

The answer to these questions is intriguing.

« Suppose you hand Owen a rattle through the slats of his crib, intentionally positioning it so that it is perpendicular to the slats. As Owen grasps the rattle, it remains pressed against the slats. No matter how hard he pulls, he cannot draw the rattle into the crib because it is stuck between two of the slats. Without hesitation Owen turns the rattle so that it, like the slats, is positioned vertically. Now, he easily pulls it into the crib.

This kind of action is somehow different from discovering the properties of the rattle itself. Clearly, it is intelligently planned; it shows great insight. Owen had to figure out a solution to the problem he was facing. He had to invent a way to solve it. He had to use a form of reflective knowledge to abstract a property of his own actions, as opposed to discovering a property of the object itself. What a marvel! This is a preliminary form of reflecting, leading in time to thinking about one's own thinking.

Such action is intelligent because it is logical. Essentially, it is as though baby goes through a reasoning process: "If I pull it this way, it gets stuck; I'll just turn it another way so it will slip through these bars." I am not proposing that the baby actually reasons his way through the dilemma as adults would in a comparable situation. I am, however, suggesting that his logic, which is initially on an action level only, eventually leads to the reasoning that approximates logic as we know it.

SOCIAL TRANSMISSION

Physical experience explains a great deal of what we know and how we come to know it. But what about the knowledge that covers such daily routines as feeding, bathing, cuddling, and playing? Or the knowledge of taking turns, as when you talk to your baby and she coos to you in response? How does she learn her mother's name? What about learning to wave bye-bye, responding to her own name, or playing pat-a-cake? Where does all this knowledge come from?

These skills all come from a single source: social learning or, more precisely, social transmission. Socially transmitted knowledge comes from people. It has been developed by the culture of the baby and is transmitted to the baby by the people around her. While a baby is interacting with people, a knowledge of the conventions of those people is being constructed that encompasses the cultural mores, values, "no-nos," folklore, music, and even rhymes of the baby's culture.

> Cultures have invented methods for creating, accumulating, and transmitting artifacts, values, and social conventions. In this way, babies are raised in a total cultural context.

Through channels of the culture (art, music, language, and education), children assimilate a great deal of socially developed knowledge, which forms a foundation for them to learn and master their own culture.

SELF-REGULATION

When my daughter Beth was about two years old, she called a swimming pool "foo na na" (at least she got the number of syllables right!). One day, we took her on vacation to Ocean City, Maryland, where she saw the ocean for the very first time. "Beeeg foo na na!" she exclaimed joyfully. Beth somehow had to deal with a new object of knowledge (ocean). Her regulating mechanism told her not to get confused: "You already know something like this (swimming pool); let's relate this new bit of knowledge to what we already know." Simple. But had she ignored this new possibility for learning a new concept, she would not have moved in the direction of higher forms of knowing. This regulating system insists that the knower somehow grapple with a new concept in an effort to achieve a higher level of knowledge.

« At every developmental point, the human mind regulates itself as it motivates the knower to attain higher forms of knowledge.

There will be times when this sort of easy regulating is challenged. For example, what if Beth had been told, "This is not a swimming pool. This is an ocean." Chances are that, at that stage of her development, she would have ignored our remark completely and maintained that it was a "big foo na na." At a somewhat later stage, perhaps, the challenge might have had an impact, and she would have been forced to create a differentiation between swimming pool and ocean.

Babies are born with an internal force that moves them in the direction of higher and higher intellectual adaptations.

The child's development has a specific direction—toward better intellectual ways of adjusting to the world of knowledge. In other words, just as the child moves from crawling to walking to running, so too does the child's ways of knowing, or "learning to know," move from simple to complex, from the physical act to the mental image to the symbol, from the here and now to the past or future, from the concrete to the abstract. Piaget has shown how this movement heads in the direction of more and more adult-like thinking.

What explains this movement toward higher and higher levels of functioning? The answer lies in the concept of equilibration, a term that comes from equilibrium or balance.

Equilibrium is a state, but equilibration is an ongoing process, one of continuous mental adjustment in an effort to strike a balance between what baby already knows and what baby is trying to understand.

Think of equilibration as an inherited force within your baby that constantly monitors activity in order to avoid confusion with every little bit of knowledge that comes along. Think of it as a regulator, a mechanism that regulates your child's learning.

 Just as a thermostat regulates heat in your house, your baby's regulator adjusts what is already known with what is encountered as a new learning experience.

First the regulator will try to relate the object of knowledge to what it already knows. If it can, then the old knowledge has been revised and extended. If it can't, then a new category of knowledge has to be constructed. In short, the regulator's role is to make sense of new learning encounters by relating the new to the old and, where it is impossible to do so, by constructing new categories of knowledge.

Our understanding all of this can be of great benefit to our children. By being aware of how the baby reacts to our correction, we can expedite this self-regulation process. There are two things to look for.

If a baby is corrected yet maintains her old way of doing things, she probably needs more time to play with the concept before she will be ready to change—just as Beth might have ignored the pool/ocean correction. That would have been a sign that she needed more time and experience with the old concept she had created. We might have shown her a small plastic wading pool (which she had), then a neighborhood-sized pool (like the one at the hotel), to focus her attention on the difference between her pool and the swimming pool. This point is very important. Children require their own amount of time to assimilate new concepts fully before they are ready to create new concepts for themselves.

On the other hand, when your correction creates a puzzle, a surprise for your child, then she is ready to learn the new concept. When baby ignores your input, it is as if your correction didn't even register. If your correction triggers a puzzled look or evokes a question, however, then you can be certain it has not only registered but has created a "disturbance," a mental disequilibrium. Aha! Now your child needs more experience with the new concept. For instance, Beth needed to discover that the ocean has waves, that its water is salty, its base is sandy, and so on. Playing at the beach reinforces her ability to distinguish between the two objects of knowledge, which helps her to construct the new concept. Like all other forms of learning, conceptual learning needs practice. After she has had enough practice (in a casual, playful setting) and has mastered the concept, she is ready to move on to another, related concept.

Think of equilibration in this way: a self-regulating process that motivates one to make sense of experience, to keep relating the new to the old until one sees the distinction and can construct a new category of knowledge.

Equilibration is an important factor in understanding and facilitating baby's intellectual development. But remember, the first three components we discussed, (maturation, physical experience, social transmission) are equally indispensable. After all, intellectual growth is a very complex topic. One factor alone does not explain it, for it is the product of the interaction among the four parts.

It is fascinating to consider the limitless possibilities of your baby's intellectual growth and development. All of this can be enhanced by your understanding, input, and encouragement—not to mention your delight at being an integral part of the process.

Now let's look at the wondrous, natural way that babies integrate the "four factors" in building knowledge—how they pull it all together!

CHAPTER TWO

Why Are the First Two Years Critical?

THE IMPORTANCE OF THE FIRST few years of life in shaping personality and emotional development has been acknowledged not only by psychologists but by the greatest thinkers and philosophers of history. Perhaps more than any other theorist, it was Sigmund Freud who awakened the world to the importance of early childhood as it affects the future personality of an individual.

More recently, the noted psychologist Erik Erikson has shown the critical importance of the first two years of life in the establishment of trust or distrust. It is now commonly acknowledged that the parents' handling of the infant—the manner in which they care for, smile, talk to, love and accept him—largely determines his attitudes and his expectations. The infant who is raised in an atmosphere of emotional support will grow to trust his environment—he'll be open to new experiences. With continued emotional support, the child will develop autonomy without experiencing unnecessary self-doubt.

But what about intellect? Do the early years play as important a role in intellectual development as they do in emotional and personality growth?

Some educational specialists, notably Dr. Benjamin Bloom of the University of Chicago, claim that mental growth roughly corresponds to brain growth. Such a connection reinforces the vital importance of the first twenty-four months of an infant's life as far as future intellectual development is concerned.

In a review of the existing studies on this subject, Bloom concluded that brain growth, like intellectual growth, occurs most rapidly during the first few years of life. A one-year-old's brain develops much more rapidly than that of a three-year-old, and a three-year-old's brain develops more rapidly than a six-year-old's. Accordingly, a one-year-old stands to profit much more from enrichment than a three-year-old or a six-year-old.

Intellectual growth occurs most rapidly—and is, ironically, nearly completed—before the child even enters school.   ◁

This does not mean that children possess all the knowledge they will have by then: of course, they will be able to learn a great deal of content in the years ahead. What it does mean is that the child's processes of knowing—his attitude about and approach to learning, his inquisitiveness, and his intense desire to satisfy his curiosity—have, for the most part, already been determined before the child enters school. In short, his intellectual processes have already been established.

Technically speaking, we can say that it is during the preschool years that the cognitive structures (the way the child organizes knowledge) as well as cognitive functions (the way intelligence is used), have been fundamentally set. This is a bold, powerful claim. It suggests that we should be making our major enrichment investment in our children *during the preschool years*, beginning as early as possible and continuing until they enter school. No other time span is more important to the development of intellectual structures or functions than the preschool years.

Only recently have we begun to grasp the full impact of early experience upon later development, although psychologists have speculated about it for over seventy years. This knowledge, which comes to us from psychology, educational psychology, and the exciting new field of psychobiology, confirms our earlier speculations that the early years are crucial to future intellectual development.

 The best summary of our present state of knowledge on this subject is a simple one: The quantity and quality of early experience is the key to future intellectual growth.

Consider the result of a classic set of animal experiments performed by Professor David Krech of the University of California at Berkeley. He studied the role of early experience on later development using laboratory rats taken from the same litter and randomly dividing them into two groups. Each group was caged and fed the same way. One group was placed in an "enriched" environment: cages with wheels that could be turned, little tunnels to run through, and things to climb over, under, around and through. The other group had none of these things. The enriched group was also allowed to explore new territories outside their cages for thirty minutes a day. In every other respect the two groups were treated equally. Three months later, the groups were sacrificed in order to explore their brains. The result was fascinating: the brains of the enriched group weighed more, had more curvatures, and contained a certain enzyme called acetylcholinesterase known to be linked to learning, remembering, and problem-solving. The smaller brains of the non-enriched group lacked this learning enzyme!

A sequel to that experiment was conducted by Professor Bernard Hymovitch, who provided enriching experiences to rats of different ages. In his experiment, however, after the enrichment/non-enrichment treatment period was over, the rats were not sacrificed; instead, they were given a kind of "rat intelligence test" in which they had to run a maze to obtain food. Two results were immediately clear: The enriched groups learned the maze much faster than the non-enriched groups, and the earlier the enrichment was introduced, the more beneficial the outcome! In addition, Hymovitch documented the importance of the *type* of enrichment used and showed that stimulus variety is directly related to future intellectual development.

These classic experiments serve to illustrate the power and the impact of an enriched environment on growth and development in the very early phases of life.

> **Interaction with an interesting and stimulating environment as early as possible has a definite impact on brain development, which in turn promotes learning ability.**

This book is certainly not meant to be a scientific treatise, but parents may find it useful to look at a few additional (and quite dramatic) findings that will help answer an important question: Even if enrichment during infancy helped baby rats to develop into better and faster learners, how do we know that enrichment in human infants could also make a difference?

Dr. Wayne Dennis studied children raised in a Teheran, Iran, orphanage in which very little human contact or mental stimulation was offered. Although these children had freedom of movement, they lacked stimulus variety—interactions with the full and varied physical and social world. When Dr. Dennis discovered these children, they had been left alone in a sterile environment practically all their lives, with disastrous results.

Sixty percent could not sit up alone until they were two years old. Eighty-five percent could not walk until age four.

Obviously, these conditions were extreme. Nonetheless, this instance of deprivation dramatically illustrates the role of early experiences, or the lack of them, upon development.

Now, a more optimistic illustration. In inner-city Milwaukee, Wisconsin, in 1971, a number of educational psychologists trained a group of mothers of newborns to play and care for their babies in ways that would help their babies develop intellectually. At four months of age the babies were brought to an infant school known as The Milwaukee Infant Education Center, where they were engaged in a variety of activities specifically designed to promote mental development. These babies were later compared with a group of babies born and raised in the same low-income area but not included in the study. The second group was comparable in age and health to the first, but their mothers had not received the same training as those of the first group; nor did these babies visit the Infant Education Center. Periodically, both groups of babies were tested. The findings were startling. By age two the enriched group had surpassed the non-enriched group significantly in cognitive attainment; by age four these differences were even more pronounced. And differences between the enriched and the non-enriched groups were still very much in evidence at the time the children turned ten.

The Milwaukee Project is only one of many studies confirming that early intervention in the lives of children has a lasting effect on their future success. Current evidence is clear: starting early—well before age three or four—puts children at an advantage and helps them to get the most from their development.

Early, stage-appropriate enriching experience is of critical importance in bolstering a child's development potential.

PREPARING FOR ENRICHING STRATEGIES

In future chapters we will be looking more closely at some specific strategies for enriching your baby's activities. Those strategies will be more likely to be effective and meaningful if we take the time to explore a few illuminating examples of the way the human brain—and specifically the very young human brain—works.

From the moment of birth, babies are able to function in remarkable ways. As you know by now, they are born with a functional set of reflexes (which we call the motor system) as well as perceptions (which we call the sensory system) that serve them extremely well. These sensori-motor systems enable them to adapt to the world around them in some limited yet functional ways. For example, when a bulky object, like a box, is pushed toward them, babies will thrust their heads back and raise their hands to protect their faces. Another interesting example is the unique way in which the brain reacts to the element of surprise. A flurry of brain activity results from an unexpected event. Baby shows attention, curiosity, and interest as a natural response to surprise.

» In 1960, Dr. Eleanor Gibson of Cornell University conducted a remarkable experiment showing that babies can perceive depth.

Thirty-six babies between the ages of six and a half and fourteen months were placed on a glass table top approximately eight feet by eight feet, half of which was blocked off with a tablecloth (although the texture of the table top itself was completely uniform). Half of the table was left uncovered, with the floor plainly visible through the glass. Placed on the table to crawl, all but three of the thirty-six babies stopped at the "deep" area and refused to go further, despite coaxing from their mothers.

Some, having reached the center, stopped and began crying—presumably wanting to get close to their mothers yet unable to do so. This demonstrated that infants can readily perceive depth.

Dr. Gibson showed that the ability to perceive depth is not learned but is somehow ingrained into the nervous system of newborns.

« In another ingenious experiment, Dr. Robert Fantz of Case Western University studied eye movements of infants only a few days old. Lying comfortably on their backs, babies were shown two patterns of the features of a human face. One pattern contained all the elements of a human face with features in the proper arrangement. The other pattern, while containing the same elements, was not arranged as a human face. The idea was to see which of the two faces attracted and kept the infants' attention longer. Invariably, infants preferred the human face over the haphazardly arranged one; apparently, infants only a few days old can distinguish one pattern as meaningful while dismissing the other as nonsense.

« Yet another important experiment involved four-month-olds who were shown two different movies on two adjacent screens simultaneously. One was a film of a toy monkey, the other, a toy donkey. Both were bouncing up and down. The difference: one had a matching soundtrack, the other did not. Once again, babies showed that they are endowed with functional perceptual abilities. They spent a significantly greater amount of time watching the movie with the soundtrack.

WHY ARE THE FIRST TWO YEARS CRITICAL? **49**

RIGHT BRAIN, LEFT BRAIN

The human brain is a wondrous instrument. Research into the relation between the brain and intellectual development has given us important insight into the cognitive preferences of babies. The two hemispheres (halves) of the brain are organized to function in different ways. The right hemisphere specializes in processing information in a simultaneous way, while the left processes it in a sequential or linear way. Speaking and counting are examples of a linear thought process; perception and music are examples of simultaneous processing.

Studies have shown that people differ in their tendency to "favor" one side of the brain as opposed to the other. Faced with the task of finding a recipe in a cookbook, for instance, some of us will scan the pages of the book convinced that we can find it quickly, while others prefer to use the index. These two different styles of doing things reflect different brain orientations. The "flipper" displays an instance of right-brain-dominated activity. The "index-scanner" illustrates the linear, left-brain-dominated way of doing things.

Which side do babies prefer? Interestingly, existing evidence suggests that infants have not yet differentiated these learning styles. However, all seem to start with a preference for right-brain kinds of actions and perceptions, preferring curvatures to angular space, responding to rhymes and music, and showing interest in patterns and wholes, not parts or segments of things. These observations point to the ability of the infant brain to perceive, react, act on and construct knowledge of the events that impact his mental life. At this very early age, baby's mind is resilient and ready to make sense of his surroundings.

Armed with this kind of knowledge, we are now ready to look at the specific strategies and methods that will help us provide the baby with opportunities for enriching experiences.

CHAPTER THREE

Approaches to Enriching Baby's Mind

MOST PARENTS WANT TO HELP their children reach important goals, and perhaps eventually even reach plateaus of achievement well above the mean. But to what extent is such heightened achievement possible for any given baby? Or, to put the issue more bluntly, can parents—or anyone else—"build" genius into children?

Some parents have been convinced that *ways* of knowing are not central to educating very young children. They believe that facts are the building blocks of intellect—and, indeed, there are some influential authors who recommend teaching infants to read and to recognize written numbers so that they may acquire a vast vocabulary for identifying things in their surroundings.

This approach is often summarized sensibly enough: "Teach specific skills—and teach them as early as possible." Teach reading and number skills, various categories of facts, musical skills, and so on. Activities are created for babies in an effort to train them to respond to specific cues in very specific ways.

Several premises underlie this method. First, parents are told, there is no inherent difference between your baby and any other baby, not even between a baby Mozart or baby Michelangelo and any other baby.

Second, if Michelangelo distinguished himself, he did so because he learned more facts. It is, apparently, the accumulation of facts that determines genius.

Therefore, the reasoning goes, the cornerstone of educational programs for the very young, including infants, should be the teaching of specific facts. And because the most efficient way to acquire facts is through the printed word, we must teach our infants to read, teach them vocabulary and number skills. For example, babies are taught to "read" words such as "mommy," "daddy," and "spaghetti," written on flash cards and presented in rapid succession. The process is repeated day in, day out until the baby learns to "read."

In this approach, reading is viewed as the critical means in advancing the intelligence of very young children. Facts constitute the building blocks of intelligence, and parents can, in effect, create geniuses of their babies by teaching them facts, reading, and number skills. The equation would look something like this:

Reading skills + number skills +
specific facts = intelligence.

This is the essence of the "superbaby" movement. Its principles are attractively simple, and that is just the problem.

BEYOND THE SUPERBABY MYTH

The widespread acceptance of these ideas may have more to do with our latent feelings of guilt than with any sound cognitive theory. Parents certainly would never knowingly deprive their children of those skills identified as the building blocks of intelligence. The superbaby approach takes an active tone—teach, and teach early—so to ignore it is to do nothing, and rob our children of potential advantage later in life! But the real question is not whether early interaction is helpful—we have seen that it is—but how valid the ideas supporting this particular theory really are.

Even the most cursory look at current scientific findings shows the superbaby notion to be simplistic and profoundly flawed. If manipulation of the early environment were the only factor in determining intellectual competence, what a different world we would live in! What a simple matter it would be to fill our schools with future Nobel laureates!

The evidence shows, however, that there are indeed fundamental genetic differences among all babies; that the Michaelangelos and Mozarts of the world do differ in profound ways from the rest of us, and in ways that have little or nothing to do with their environment; and that any recipe for creating geniuses through the inculcation of facts and figures denies the exquisitely complicated interactive dance between the child's innate structures and her surroundings.

There is no baby on earth exactly like yours. There is no substitute for identifying your baby's current methods of knowing and promoting meaningful experiences from within that framework.

 While we are unable to manufacture genius, that is certainly no reason to limit ourselves to a passive approach.

Enrichment of the natural, spontaneous processes of intelligence during infancy can sharpen infants' intellectual potential and endow them with the desire to know—a much more meaningful gift than any pre-arranged list designed for rote memorization.

We must nurture the *ways* of knowing—the marvelous processes of learning and understanding. Remember, to enhance the natural processes of curiosity, discovery, and inventiveness in our young children is not to hurry them. Rather, it is to make their intellectual life more interesting, more rewarding, less frustrating, and certainly more fun.

Enriching the fundamental intellectual processes during infancy and toddlerhood (and continuing to do so throughout the preschool years) encourages the construction of an intellectual foundation upon which all future knowledge is based.

My own perception of the purpose of educating the very young child is certainly not to raise a "superbaby"—one who has been trained to perform rote skills—but to provide a supporting, encouraging, and warm environment in which the processes of intelligence are permitted to develop. The self-selected, spontaneous activities of the baby are most rewarding in an atmosphere of play, activity, and fun. The purpose is not to accelerate the rate at which babies attain various stages in mental development; it is to influence the quality of mental activity in each stage so that the brilliant, ceaseless pageant of intellect has a chance to proceed in its proper course.

« This debate brings to mind the three-year-old boy who impressed adults with his ability to "read" the word "booster rocket" while pointing to a picture of one. The fact that the child can make the association means nothing in terms of what has been learned. No one would suggest that this youngster knows a thing about the principles of rocketry, boosters, or stellar navigation!

We refer to such instances of learning as empty verbalisms—words devoid of meaning. Equipping children with empty verbalisms may impress the uninitiated parent and the "audience," but it is a meaningless, useless form of learning.

» Or consider the one-year-old son of a colleague of mine. Not too long ago I accompanied both of them on a summer motor trip of several hundred miles; my friend kept pointing to cows grazing in the countryside and repeating the word "cow."  He believed that if a word were repeated and associated with the object it represented over and over again, a child could actually learn that word's meaning. My friend must have pointed and repeated the word "cow" dozens of times. When we reached our destination, the child looked at his father's index finger. "Cow!" he said proudly.

Yes: children can learn simple associations between words and objects. But even if they connect a word with the right object, it is still not known what else—if anything—they have learned.

Superbaby training programs, as we have seen, teach babies to respond in specific ways to specific stimulus situations, not unlike the one-year-old boy we just discussed. Some trainers have impressed parents by teaching their babies to respond to cards containing varying numbers of dots in different configurations. For example, baby Jennifer is trained to pick the card that has the most dots. The trainer then concludes that Jennifer has learned something about the concept of number; her parents are convinced she has superior learning powers!

Unfortunately, training babies to perform these kinds of tasks is useless. It is extremely seductive, though; it lulls parents into believing that their child has mastered something that will advance her intelligence. But this kind of learning tends to be short-lived and is of no consequence in the child's overall future intellectual development.

> **We should not be concerned with equipping babies with end results, ready-made facts, or simple associations.**

Little is gained if a child knows which of two cards has more dots on it or turns out to be the first on the block to speak or read. If these things happen without prodding, fine. It is pointless to push your baby into artificial learning situations, situations that emphasize achievement based on rote learning. This constitutes rushing a child. Young children must pay too high an emotional price when they are inappropriately and immaturely pushed to achieve.

HOW IMPORTANT IS READING?

For so many, intelligence is synonymous with the ability to use "the word." But a baby who is, say, one month old has no words. He has perceptions and actions. And it is through these, and especially combinations of these, that he constructs knowledge of what is. The terrible mistake we so often make is to equate a baby's intelligence with the ability to speak, and later, with the ability to read and write. Reading and writing often take on disproportionate importance in the way we evaluate the very early development of the child.

Some parents have been convinced that reading to their babies, and even their unborn children, is important to future development. Somehow the unborn baby is supposed to absorb this extremely complex symbolic activity even before he is born! The less zealous protagonists of reading to unborn babies claim that at least the fetus is getting used to your voice. If there is any truth to this notion, then your everyday conversations with people should do the trick.

Reading to an unborn child is, quite simply, an utter waste of time. Better to spend time preparing for his arrival, learning about his physical development, and attending to the physical, nutritional, and psychological condition of the mother. Once he is born, you should concentrate on providing love, care, and social and mental interaction.

Much later on, reading takes on great significance. It enables the child to speed up mental processes and accomplish actions symbolically as opposed to actively. It enables the mind to soar, to imagine objects and events that are not physically present to the reader. It frees the mind from the confining here and now. So reading is important—but not in infancy.

And yet we should recognize that even reading, this symbolic way of knowing, is also active. Action is the mother of intelligence, not words. The baby, child, adolescent, adult—no matter—has to act in order to know. In infancy, this action is physical; in toddlerhood the possibility of representing actions through symbols (such as words) and signs (such as stop signs) becomes a reality. Later, actions are represented through more complicated symbols and signs. As we approach adolescence, the action of manipulating symbolic systems (while doing algebra, for instance) becomes possible. But it all starts with the infant. First the baby must master reflex actions, then differentiate them from another, then integrate them, coordinating them in new arrangements. Only when she has had enough experience performing these coordinations and differentiations to the point where she has a practical intelligence—an intelligence of here and now, of concrete objects and her interactions with them—can she graduate to the world of the sign and the symbol. Be patient. After eighteen months or so, and certainly by her second birthday, she will be able to do just that.

ACTIVITY

Having taken a look at some of the benefits of early experience and the disadvantages of the superbaby approach, we can now ask, What is an enriching environment? What is the key ingredient in mental development? The answer, in a word, is activity.

Professor J. M. Hunt of the University of Illinois made a painstaking review of the existing literature and concluded that stimulus variety was the crucial ingredient in mental development. His broad conclusion was that, within limits, the more varied the stimulus to which a baby is exposed, the greater the benefits will be.

Applying this principle, however, is not always simple. There must be a limit to both the kind and the amount of stimulation, or one can easily overstimulate a child, causing emotional harm. The goal is to provide an appropriate amount of stimulating, enriching experience. For optimum benefits, one has to strike a balance between the baby's stage of cognitive growth and the kind and quantity of stimulation.

How do we do this? Well, as it turns out, the parental impulse we discussed earlier in this chapter—the desire to raise "genius" or "gifted" children—is actually a constructive one. There are, after all, children who grow up to achieve great things. Most parents would like very much to learn more about the early life of these children! By studying the families in which such people grew up, we find that the ideas of balance and challenge we have been discussing are a major part of successful parenting.

HOW THE GIFTED ARE RAISED

Professor Benjamin Bloom of the University of Chicago recently concluded an ambitious survey of 120 Americans considered to be among the top mathematicians, sculptors, neurologists, swimmers and tennis players in the United States. He found that the single most significant factor in each child's development was the parents, all of whom shared four key characteristics. They understood the importance of

1. *Very early play and encouragement.* They provided rich environments in which their children could explore the outside world as well as their own abilities. In so doing, they assured ample opportunity for the children to initiate their own play. These parents understood that learning must take place in the act of play; that it must be fun and deeply enjoyable to the child.

2. *The home environment in motivating their children.* They created wholesome surroundings with different kinds of interesting interactions in which children were able to explore their individual interests to the fullest and continue in their self-chosen activities. In all cases, parents served as models of motivated, determined people.

3. *Their child's self-chosen interest as his or her own priority.* Once their child reached school age, they made every effort to continue supporting him/her in self-initiated, self-chosen interests.

4. *Their parental responsibility in their children's development.* They contributed to their children's remarkable success by remaining open-minded while encouraging independent thinking and free
exploration.

The parents of extremely bright children—children
who excel in a variety of talents, from music to science,
from art to mathematics, from athletics to neurology—
have these traits in common. They provide a warm, loving, accepting home environment with varied opportunities for meaningful interaction and an abundance of
people, physical objects, and events. They stress independent thinking as opposed to programmed teaching
of ready-made facts. They encourage free exploration,
manipulation, self-initiated play, investigation, and
problem-solving, all of which are paramount to their
joyful, challenging parenting process.

PIAGET: EDUCATING THE INTELLECT

This, by the way, is completely in keeping with the position taken by Piaget. The goals of education, he believed, should stress independent thinking, discovery,
and invention. Writing of the relation between adult
society and the to-be-educated child, he states that we
can no longer afford for this relationship to be unidirec-
tional—with adult society giving out ready-made knowledge for children to absorb and repeat in the right context. "The child," wrote Piaget, "no longer tends to
approach the state of adulthood by receiving reason and
the rules of right action ready-made, but by achieving
them with its own effort and personal experience; in
turn, society expects more of its new generation than

mere imitation: it expects enrichment." (*Piaget*, 1972, p. 138.)

Transmitting a set body of knowledge does not produce creative people. To improve society, the goals of education need to exceed mere repetition and imitation; they must stress independent inquiry. This emphasis is particularly crucial in view of our era of passing fads and the many pressures to conform that our children will face.

▷ **The ability to be critical, to verify, to be prepared to reject the first idea that is presented if necessary—this is what we must instill in our children, and indeed in our society as a whole.**

To accomplish all this requires an attitude on the part of parents that puts a premium on the spontaneous activity of the child, activity that is encouraged and guided by a knowledgeable parent or caregiver.

It is simply not normal for babies to be passive recipients of stimulation. They should be

» acting upon objects and events, not merely spectating

» choosing and initiating the types of interactions, not being subjected to traditional curriculum filtered down from elementary school

» doing the performing, not having the performing done for or to them

LESSONS FROM INFANT DAY CARE

When it comes to general guidelines for enriching babies' and young children's intellects, we can learn a great deal from professional educators who design enriching environments to promote beneficial activities. I am speaking, of course, of infant day care center educators.

Following are some suggestions professionals in this field have for caregivers and teachers in these settings. In many ways, they are appropriate to parents, as well.

Accept that individual children will differ in temperament and approach; do not expect one child to react to the same challenge in the same way another might.

Offer toys that are appropriate to age and stage.

Avoid interruptions and corrections.

Smile; make eye contact.

Show delight when the child succeeds.

Don't give complicated instructions. Make sure the language you use is comprehensible.

Be prepared for new variations on uses of playthings that you (or others) may not have anticipated. Just be sure to keep baby's safety in mind at all times.

Remember that the child's showing puzzlement at a new concept is a good sign.

Help the child master activities by encouraging repetition.

Bear in mind where the child has given up in the past with a certain plaything. Next time, help the child resume at that point.

When appropriate, direct the child to a parallel—but simpler—activity.

Demonstrate by playing with the toy yourself first.

Provide the next level of challenge with a toy or concept before the child becomes bored with it. (This may take some practice on your part to learn exactly when the restlessness is likely to set in.)

Encourage new associations and combinations.

Encourage cooperation with others by showing delight at instances of sharing and playing with companions.

Be available to share discoveries, consult on problems, and offer support—but don't do the playing *for* the child. The best approach is to maintain a presence such that the baby knows you are there to appeal to if necessary.

Listen—both to actual words and to more subtle types of communication, such as glances and body language.

Avoid showing discouragement or impatience at instances of what you may consider "failure" at a given task. (Doing so may actually pose developmental obstacles for the child.) Instead, put the accent on positive reinforcement and unconditional affection.

Highlight those activities, friendships, and playthings that have been demonstrated to be of interest to the child. (Why focus on that for which the child has demonstrated he has no interest?)

CHAPTER FOUR

The Stages of Babyhood

To UNDERSTAND THE INTRICACIES of intellectual development and to gain a full appreciation of the task of enriching your baby's mind, we must take a moment to discuss the concept of stages—those through which your baby (and all babies) travel.

 Mental development progresses in phases and stages.

Contrary to popular belief, intellectual development is not a linear progression steadily ascending to the top. In reality, mental development between birth and adulthood can best be described as a spiral with four major turns, each constituting a distinct way of knowing—a phase. Of course, it is the first phase that is of greatest interest to us; here is the complete list.

- Sensori-motor Intelligence—birth through 2 years.

- Preoperational Thought—2 through 7-8 years

- Concrete Operational Thought—7-8 through 12-14.

- Formal Operational Thought—14 on.

The sensori-motor period constitutes a way of know-ing restricted to what is present at the moment—to knowing through the senses and through physical action. A form of practical intelligence, sensori-motor knowing enables babies to adapt to their immediate environment. Handicapped by the lack of a mature symbolic system, the sensori-motor baby is simply stuck in the here and now; unable to make words and images stand for real objects and events, he can understand only on a sensory and motoric plane. This is particularly true during the first year of life.

During the second year, and certainly by the end of that year, a child begins to construct a symbolic system, displaying the ability to mentally represent objects and events in their absence. This includes the use of simple words and phrases to speak of things not perceived (mostly wants and needs), images of absent objects (appreciating the fact that disappearing objects are behind something), and abbreviated movements (using hand motions to convey ideas).

By the end of the second year, intellect starts to soar. As the symbolic system develops, it enables the child to image something, imitate someone, talk about an absent event. A new and wonderful world of knowing opens up with the onset of the symbolic system. Now the child can offer reasons for things, although, by our standards, the rationale or intuition of a two-year-old is often entirely wrong! The process is a gradual one, showing that the appearance of mental abilities doesn't sprout overnight, but evolves over time and with experience.

Each phase, period or stage builds on the the preceding one, advancing the child to a new and more elaborate, flexible, and adult-like way of thinking.

> A stage, then constitutes a manner of knowing—a way of understanding, a particular process of making sense. Children the world over undergo stages in order, although the speed with which they complete them may vary.

Stages are sequential, following one another in an orderly manner.

Note that humans pass through the four periods I outlined earlier (as well as the stages within them) without skipping. One must attain one stage before going on to the next, and this progression of attainments cannot be altered.

It is quite reasonable to expect children who are the same age to function on different stages of intelligence. Given normal heredity, it is safe to say that differences in the rate of development depend upon a child's interactive experience. Assuming normal and similar maturation of babies, families who provide an abundance of love, care, and mental enrichment enjoy children who are happy, content, curious, alert, quick learners, initiators, and, in general, "explorers" and manipulators of things.

> Between birth and the end of the second year, babies undergo six specific stages.

Envision the six sensori-motor stages of infancy as a spiral with six turns, each turn a little larger than the one below (preceding) it. A later stage builds on preceding ones; subsuming, encompassing, and assimilating them onto itself.

STAGE I

« Stage I babies (birth through the first month), are restricted to the use of reflex actions. Because their knowledge system is tied to such ways of knowing as grasping, sucking, eye-movements, etc., things are known only if they trigger these reflex actions.

For example, when a nipple touches the area of a baby's mouth, sucking begins. Such knowledge, or more precisely, such adaptations, are simply survival instincts.

Moreover, these reflexes are not integrated with one another. They act independently from one another. Sucking and grasping, for example, are not put together into a coherent single action.

STAGE II

» Stage II babies (one through four months) develop a way of knowing that is superior to the rigid, fragmented way of knowing of Stage I babies: they learn to coordinate one reflex action with another, creating new action patterns that are more organized, elaborate and wholistic. Stage II ushers in the possibility for acquiring new patterns of behavior as a result of integrating one act with another, then undoing the integration to integrate acts in an entirely new way. The ability to integrate and differentiate actions enables the baby to construct new way of doing things, new ways of organizing and adapting to reality. This expands the realm of learning, enabling the baby to start "playing" and "imitating."

The baby's actions are oriented toward himself at this stage and are at first produced unintentionally. Once produced, actions can be repeated. Every time baby repeats the action, new objects are incorporated into his scheme of the action. Coordinating hand and mouth, following objects with his eyes, turning his head in the direction of sound, producing sounds or vocalizing, imitating sounds he could already produce, and other elements of early play are all examples of coordinating and organizing reflexes and primitive perceptions.

STAGE III

« The ability to exercise skills by manipulating the external world of objects is the distinguishing characteristic of the Stage III baby (four to eight months). Baby can now reproduce an outcome that she had caused accidentally and found interesting. For example, when she thrashes her legs around in her crib, baby Christy notices that the mobile suspended above her moves. She thrashes around again, trying to make the mobile move once more. If she is successful, she will repeat the process again and again. The baby actually enjoys repeating the pattern of behavior she has just learned.

Baby Christy's behavior is exciting for two reasons. First, it is directed toward an object outside the baby's own body; second, the action is repeated. If Christy perceives a relationship between her act and the resulting event, she must be forming a primitive but practical understanding of cause and effect, or the means-ends principle. Doing *this*, she has learned, produces *that*. The Stage III baby has an enormous ability to learn new ways of doing things.

STAGE IV

» After the rapid learning of Stage III, the Stage IV baby (eight to twelve months) is busy consolidating her past learning and applying it to new situations. This is a time of reconciling the attainments of the past and extending them to new and different situations. In this stage a number of major attainments are being perfected, beginning with the concept of means-ends relations. The infant now shows an intentional, as opposed to accidental, selection of means to accomplish preestablished goals, and is developing his concept of space and time more fully. On a practical level only, concepts such as "in," "out," "behind," "through," etc., are understood. This helps the infant attain understanding of the concept of the permanence of objects. In the previous stage, baby could only search for a disappearing object visually; now, he begins to search manually! This important development shows the child's advancement in understanding that objects can go out of sight without totally vanishing from the world.

Peek-a-boo becomes intensely interesting in this stage; the game gives baby a chance to confirm this new understanding. Imitating has progressed to the point where the baby can reproduce an action that involves parts of her body she cannot see. Anticipation—associating certain events when they are preceded by others—is also being perfected. When a sequence is disrupted, the element of surprise enters into her world.

STAGE V

« Now a toddler, the Stage V child (twelve to eighteen months) can experiment and solve problems, initially through trial and error, but later on, quite efficiently. She intentionally and systematically varies an action to discover how changes in her actions affect outcomes. She understands that not only she but other people and objects can cause things to happen. She has constructed some idea of time, of space, and of how objects fit in and out of things. She knows that if an object has been moved from one hiding place to another, she'll find it by looking where it was last seen. And she can imitate novel acts—acts that she has not imitated before.

Because she is beginning to develop the capacity to represent objects and events mentally through images, words, and abbreviated actions, she is freed from a knowledge system that was restricted to what she could touch, see, hear, smell, and taste. Now she is able to know things by imaging them. When it is completed, what an incredible accomplishment that will be! Stage V is the beginning of the end of sensori-motor intelligence. Over the next year or so, the symbolic system will have evolved to the point where an entirely new age of knowing becomes possible, the age of the wonderful, magical, make-believe world of early childhood.

STAGE VI

» In this last stage of the sensori-motoric period (eighteen to twenty-four months), the symbolic system is so well developed that children can solve problems without resorting to the trial and error experimentation of the Stage V child; they can run through the solution to a problem mentally and then solve it. Stage VI is a transition period, one that, upon its completion, will hurl the child into the world of thought. Parents delight in witnessing the phenomenon of insight: when confronted with a problem, the child shows little or no physical groping before hitting on a solution. As this period ends, a new mode of mental activity characterized by a magical, intuitive, and egocentric kind of thought begins—the thought of the preschooler.

CHAPTER FIVE

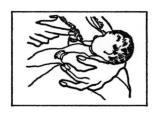

Stage I
(Birth to 1 Month)

WHEN WE LOOK AT THE PROCESS of a baby's early mental development, we often bring with us certain preconceptions and set attitudes. Of course, one certainly would not want a new parent to be *completely* objective about his or her baby, considering that the bonding process itself is a vital and uniquely personal matter. But certain pieces of "received wisdom" that are quite separate from the parental instincts to protect or care for a child seem to be handed down from generation to generation. Many of these ideas can be traced to the opinions of "experts" of years past, and have now taken on the status of folk wisdom concerning babies.

True or False?

- Newborns cannot hear until four weeks old.
- Newborns cannot see until approximately seven weeks old.
- Infants are unaware of their surroundings until eight weeks old.
- Singing or talking to infants is not important until the twelfth week.

It is not uncommon even today to hear these "facts" exchanged among parents. But the statements are all false.

These, along with other "infants can't" myths handed down and accepted for ages, are simply meaningless standards. (Many parents suspect as much as they watch their "sightless" infant show signs of intense interest in close objects.) So much has been written about the weaknesses, foibles, and frailties of infants that it is not surprising how readily such notions are accepted.

It is true that human infants, among all animal species, are the most dependent upon their caretakers, and that they remain dependent for the longest period of time. One might not think that human babies are born with a remarkable sensori-motor system and are superbly equipped to adapt to—and meaningfully interact with—their surroundings from the instant of birth. Yet this is so.

Unfortunately, the common misconceptions we have long accepted account for a double tragedy. First, a newborn's parents have such low expectations of their baby's capabilities that they simply don't bother to offer any special enrichment. Consequently, they miss out on the joys that come with observing and aiding their child's earliest development. Second, as a result of his parents' low expectations and their failure to provide more than mere "bodily" attention, the baby is deprived of the significant early enrichment that can mean so much intellectually later in life.

Realization of a few simple yet vital facts of life and birth can—and will—make a wonderful difference in your attitude toward early parenting.

WHAT A NEWBORN KNOWS

» Your baby is born with an innately equipped sensori-motor system that permits immediate adaptation to people and to physical surroundings. Let's examine a newborn's capabilites—first in the area of sensory abilities, then in motoric skills.

SENSORY ABILITIES

From birth, and certainly by the first week of life, your baby is able to

- Smell—fully developed sense at birth.
- Taste—fully developed sense at birth
- Focus—best from a distance of seven to eight inches with the object directly in front of her face.
- Discern patterns—preferring contrast, contour, and curvy lines over geometric (angular) shapes.
- Stop reacting—to irritating stimuli after prolonged exposure. This helps the baby shut out disturbing sights and sounds.
- Pay attention—to location of sound (however briefly).
- Regard human faces briefly—preferring them to other objects.
- Stop sucking—to attend to something.
- Respond—to all elements of sound, including pitch, loudness, timbre, and rhythm.

MOTORIC SKILLS

In addition to sensory powers, your baby is born with an operational motoric system, which is the basis of much of his future learning and development. At the heart of this system is a set of reflexes that accounts for baby's survival. These reflexes include: crying, sound-making, sneezing, coughing, sucking, eye movements (blinking, focusing, tracking), grasping, and swallowing. These actions are reflexive because they are set off by objects or events in the baby's surroundings. If, for example, you stroke your son's cheek or the area near his mouth with your hand, his head turns and his tongue moves toward your hand. Once he finds your hand, he begins sucking. Or, if you shine a small light into his eyes, or clap your hands in front of his face, he will close his eyes tightly.

SELECTED REFLEXES OF NEWBORNS

Reflex	Description
Automatic Walking	Walking movements with feet when supported to a standing position.
Babinski	Toes spread out when soles of feet are stimulated.
Blinking	Eyes closes tightly when bridge of her nose gently tapped.
Crawling	Turns head to side, lifts self with arms, makes crawling motion when placed on tummy.
Grasping	Grasps very firmly at finger placed in palm.
Moro	Head drops back, arms fly out to

the side, and fingers extend when sudden noise or contact is made, or when newborn is "dropped" in the air a few inches and held again.

Rooting   Turns in the direction of the stimulus when cheeks are stroked.

Sucking   Sucking begins when baby's lips or mouth area are stroked.

At birth, these reflexes are isolated, underdeveloped, and clumsy. For the first month or so, they seem to function independently of one another. For instance, the grasping reflex is not connected with sucking, and the baby does not seem to have any awareness of stimulus events that trigger his reflexes. In fact, the baby does not have any awareness that objects exist separate from himself.

In addition, the reflex actions operate on an action level only; that is to say, in a mechanical way, without intention. Gradually baby begins to coordinate various reflexes with one another, as when he grasps a rattle and "gums" or sucks it. However, this type of coordination is not expected until the end of the first month of life. Coordination of reflex actions signals the beginning of a new stage of intellect, that which we refer to as Stage II.

Of course, not all reflex actions play an important role in intellectual development. While grasping, sucking, and eye-movements are the stuff from which intelligence is built, sneezing and coughing do absolutely nothing to promote mental growth.

Now: how does a baby gain knowledge through these reflex actions and elementary sensory perceptions?

SENSORI-MOTOR INTELLIGENCE

In Stage I, the first month of life, your baby is restricted to the use of reflex actions. Because her knowledge system is restricted to such ways of knowing as grasping, sucking, and eye-movements, things are known only if they trigger these reflex actions. If an object cannot be grasped, placed in the mouth, or looked at closely in many different positions, then from a practical point of view—your baby's—it may as well not exist.

It bears repeating that the knowledge we are examining is not a knowledge that is represented mentally. Rather, it is supremely functional. In this stage, the ability to represent objects by imaging them or symbolizing them is utterly foreign. For now, knowledge is limited to reflexes and primitive perceptions as they interact with the to-be-known object. It can be said that in Stage I, baby's major accomplishment, if not her preoccupation during her waking, alert hours (about one hour in every ten), is to exercise her reflexes.

The Stage I enrichment objective is to refine these reflex actions and to ready them for the next step in mental development—coordinating reflex actions with one another.

Babies have an intrinsic desire to exercise the skills they develop. Mastery of skills seems to be an integral part of their mental lives. Consider this fascinating experiment.

» Infants were situated in front of a screen and were given a pacifier device hooked up to a focusing mechanism. If the infant sucked on the pacifier rapidly, a picture on the screen would come into focus. If, on the other hand, the infant stopped sucking, the picture went out of focus. Under these conditions, the infants learned very quickly and, in fact, seemed to derive pleasure from "solving" this little puzzle. They actually speeded up their sucking to focus the picture! Then, when the experimenters reversed the task so that it was necessary to stop sucking in order to focus the image, the infants learned to control that situation as well!

This ingenious experiment is only one among many showing the wonderfully resilient nature of the infant mind. Even in the first few days of life, newborns are ready and able to exercise their known skills and try making sense of—and mastering—their surroundings. More importantly, their innate desire to know more invariably leads them to coordinate one skill with another.

In an earlier chapter, I pointed out that the integration of skills, their decoupling, and their reintegration in new combinations is the key to understanding mental growth. Yet mental processes do not take place in a vacuum. They are applied to specific objects and events in an effort to construct knowledge. As babies interact with objects around them, they begin to construct some basic know-how of the fundamental categories of knowledge. What are these categories of knowledge?

TYPES OF KNOWLEDGE

Reflex actions and primitive reflexes are ways of knowing, means by which babies come to know the world in which they live. Focusing, visually tracking, reaching, grasping, and sucking are all functions of the intellect. These functions, or actions, must be directed toward some intellectual content area.

« For example: as your baby holds your finger, she is applying the grasping function to it. In doing so, she is discovering properties of your finger, such as its size, warmth, and feel, thereby learning about your finger as an object, a "content area." In other words, as she applies her reflex actions to a wide variety of objects and events (content areas), she constructs knowledge.

Piaget, following the insights of the renowned philosopher Emanuel Kant, proposed that the most important content areas for the development of the human mind were object, time, space, and causality. It's fascinating to discover how infant intelligence is applied to these content areas and how knowledge is constructed from each.

THE OBJECT CONCEPT

The object concept in its mature form refers to the knowledge or belief that an object (a person, thing, or place) will continue to exist even though we are not in direct perceptual contact with it. For instance, I don't see my car right now, yet I know (or believe) that it exists. I don't have to sense it directly to know it is still in existence.

Infants are not born with this ability. They must construct it bit by bit. Normally, it takes approximately ten months for newborns to begin searching manually for a hidden object, a good indication that they know the object continues to exist even though they can't see it, and thus possess a mature object concept.

During the first month of life, infants show no sign whatsoever of this concept, and, what's more, cannot differentiate themselves from other objects in their surroundings. If they did, they could establish the notion that objects have a certain permanence, independent of their own. But since this differentiation is not yet made, Stage I babies cannot construct the concept of the permanence of objects. Similarly, infants' concepts of time, space, and causality are nonexistent, developing only as a result of maturation and experience.

ENRICHMENT: GENERAL GUIDELINES

The limited, uncoordinated reflex and perceptual system with which your baby is born requires maturation and experience in order to become fully functional. How can you help enhance the process?

First, be aware of differences between her abilities and yours. For instance, baby's eyes are almost half the size of yours. It is because they are not fully developed that she can only focus on objects that are seven to eight inches away from her face.

> When trying to attract baby's attention with visual cues, be certain that you stay within the seven-to-eight-inch range, directly in front of her face, and use bold print objects with great contrast (black and white is an excellent choice).

Even when your baby does see an object, she will have difficulty making sense of it. This is due, in part, to lack of experience and her still-developing nervous system. As yet, she is not physiologically equipped to transmit the visual image to the brain readily and speedily, and even if she could, her lack of experience with the object would not permit her brain to do anything with it. The net result is that she responds more slowly to a visual stimulus than you do. What appears to be a visual limitation may, in fact, be a remarkable built-in mechanism for ensuring that baby perceives only those things that are absolutely necessary for survival: your face, your hands, or the nipple.

Later, between four and six months of age, when there is a need to reach for objects, her eyes will converge on objects that are farther away. Her visual system, as well as her ability to coordinate her vision with her hand and arm movements, will also have matured by that time.

Second, respect the delicate balance between enrichment and your baby's emotional, physical, and mental state. To take full advantage of an enrichment opportunity, your baby needs to be calm, alert, and content. Offer just enough interaction to create interest while avoiding possible overstimulation, which could lead to chaos and confusion. Psychologists have shown us that babies will turn off stimulation by falling asleep!

▷ The optimal approach is one in which an atmosphere of relaxed warmth, love, and caring prevails—where activities are enjoyed in a spirit of fun and guided play—where respect for baby's comfort is never compromised.

Perspective is key: we are mentors, not zealots; we are providers of interesting, engaging interactions, not givers of ready-made knowledge; we are designers of play environments conducive to fun, discovery, and invention, not instructors of specific facts or skills. We must always stand guard against our desire to see our baby excel by keeping her state and interest as the focal point of our interactions.

Finally, let's remember that whatever we do must be done with the baby's safety in mind.

CREATING AN ENRICHING ENVIRONMENT

» *Bold, contrastingly sharp patterns for baby's crib sheet.*
Babies prefer to look at human faces. So why not use bed sheets, quilts, and bumpers that have large patterns of faces printed on them? Even if presented as abstract drawings, they will do just fine.

« Bold contrastingly sharp patterns for baby to look at and later play with.

• Make a large banner using a solid color of felt or flannel. Cut out varying shapes and patterns from other colored swatches of material. Attach velcro to the backs of these pieces and place them on the solid banner to create an interesting pattern or picture. Remember: this is the time to emphasize contours, patterns and contrasts.

• Change the colors, shapes, and designs as the baby grows older. Eventually, at around sixteen or seventeen months, your baby will be ready to help you place the pieces on your banner. Later in development, the banner can be used as an aid in teaching shapes and colors.

• During the early months of life, hang this banner approximately two feet from your infant's crib so that it can be seen clearly.

« A crib bumper with good color contrasts.

• This is important for enriching eye-movements, as well as for safety and protection.

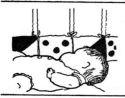

« A black and white checkerboard blanket containing twelve to sixteen squares with different shapes and figures in each square.

• Babies' attention is drawn to contrasting hues. So this kind of blanket or quilt will be a source of interest for the baby. Use this blanket when you put baby on her stomach for a few minutes. This will strengthen back and neck muscles.

> • Do *not* place an infant stomach-down (or in any position) on a bean-bag cushion; the baby may suffocate. Unfortunately, many have; these cushions are recognized to be extremely dangerous and completely inappropriate for use with infants.

» *A ribbon or elastic tied across the crib rails to which various objects and small toys are tied.*
Examples:

  • A crumpled piece of aluminum foil.
  • A 3" by 5" piece of colorful cloth.
  • A plastic spoon.
Baby will delight at looking at these objects as they move about. For visual variety, change the position of the toys and objects, and periodically change them altogether. Be certain all objects are firmly attached to the elastic and always choose soft, safe objects (light enough so that if they accidentally fall on baby she won't get hurt, yet large enough so they can't be swallowed). Make sure that the entire ribbon of objects is dangling at the right length (between seven to eight inches from baby).

« A mobile.
You can buy or make one. Either way, a mobile should have the baby in mind, not the adult. Most mobiles look interesting when *we* look at them at *our* eye level. But remember, your baby is on her back most of the time, getting a bottom view of the mobile. It should look interesting when viewed from the bottom as well as the side. Some mobiles contain little motors to turn them steadily, others have music boxes that chime a simple melody. Whether you make or buy one, remember that boldness, contrast, contour, print, and angle of vision from the baby's perspective are very important considerations.

There is certainly nothing wrong with a simple mobile at this stage. Decorate a paper plate with a black and white bull's eye design, then suspend it from the ceiling with a ribbon. This will be more than adequate.

« A hand puppet.
Since human faces are so interesting to babies, try to make or buy a puppet that has human features. On occasion, it's fun to play with your baby while using a puppet. Remember, your baby's head is disproportionately large in relation to the rest of her body, so when picking her up, propping her up or carrying her, make sure that you provide support for her neck and the back of her head.

» *Common kitchen objects: plastic measuring spoons, cups.*

Occasionally you can put on a variety show. Simply show these objects to baby for a minute or two while talking to her. Soon, after daily repetitions of this process, baby starts reaching for familiar objects. This will be your signal that she has entered Stage II.

» *When playing with baby, place a finger into each of her hands and gently pull her into a sitting position.*

You will notice that your baby's arms and legs move when she gets excited and that when you place your finger in the palm of her hand, she will tend to grasp it. How strong her grip is during the first month of life! To nurture this reflex action, place soft objects and toys into her hand: a hand towel, a large wooden spoon, a rattle, or a large plastic ring. All of these objects, which provide a variety of shapes, textures, and color, can be used to encourage the grasping and sucking reflexes.

» *Talk, sing, play soft music.*

Toward the end of baby's first month of life, she makes tiny throaty sounds and responds to human voices. But just because she can't talk back or sing along does not mean that you shouldn't talk or sing to her—lots. When you do, her vocal activity can increase and you are participating in the earliest beginnings of language development! Since her sense of hearing is finely tuned, use your voice to soothe her when she is fussy.

« Touch baby's cheeks.
At first your baby will respond wildly when either cheek is touched. Later he will turn to whichever cheek is being stimulated. Does he respond differently when his cheek is rubbed rather than stroked gently? Stroking stimulates the searching reflex, triggering the drive to eat. Touch his cheek with the satin edge of a blanket, then with your skin, a sweater, a rattle, a rubber ball. Your skin may set off the most searching, as he begins to associate skin with the nourishment and affection that often follow a touch. This enhances the baby's early development of accommodation—fitting his behavior to the object he is in contact with.

« Touch your baby's lips.
Gently touch your fingers to your baby's lips. Does he start to suck? As a variation, try brushing lips with a soft toy. Your baby is developing the ability to discriminate between nipples, fingers, toys, and so on. This activity also helps your baby to gain control over the sucking reflex. In Stage II, baby may start to lick rather than suck. This is a progression from simply sucking.

« Massage baby on a daily basis.
This is highly recommended; it stimulates baby's muscles and makes them more responsive. Massaging is a wonderful way to awaken baby's muscles when he wakes up from a nap. The touching also builds a bond. Holding, touching, hugging, and massaging baby are as essential to baby's mind as they are to baby's emotional development. Do this every day while talking, singing, or playing music.

A WORD ABOUT LANGUAGE

As we have already seen, reading in the first two years of life is, in my view, an overrated activity. But what about language? That, as it turns out, is a very different story. Let's take a look at language development in the first two years of life. What should we expect during these two formative years and what should our role be in it?

The very word *infant* derives from the Latin *infans*, which means without language. So why bother with a discussion of language here? The answer is a straightforward one: while babies can't use language much to express themselves, they nevertheless are forming the foundation for doing so. What does this foundation consist of?

In the first year of her life, you can expect your baby to vocalize; that means the baby will be uttering certain vocal sound that are the precursors of language. These vocalizations amount to the baby's announcement that she can produce speech sounds.

Four distinct types of vocalizations have been observed in all normal babies, regardless of the culture in which they are raised. Universally, babies are first capable of *crying and grunting*. Crying is usually associated with some sort of arousal or need state such as hunger, thirst, or pain. This first stage lasts about three months.

Near the end of the third month, the baby begins to produce utterances best described as *cooing*. The baby takes up the prolonged vowel-like sounds with great enthusiasm; this is where we might start guessing that the baby is trying to communicate.

By about the sixth month of life, the baby enters a third stage of language development, *babbling*. Babbling differs from cooing in that it involves a combination of vowel and consonant sounds producing utterances like "mamamama." Interestingly, we still cannot distinguish between an American baby and a Chinese baby at this stage strictly based on their babbling. Babies the world over babble much the same way. Soon pitch variation begins to appear in the babbling.

Not until the fourth stage, with the production of *patterned speech*, do children actually begin to tune into speech sounds and patterns in their native language, the language being spoken around them.

By their first birthday, babies use intonation to indicate commands and, later on, to indicate questions using single *words*. At this point, you might notice a child's gradual approximations approaching recognizable words: from *dodi* to *goggie* to *doggie*. Such meaningful words don't usually appear until the first birthday.

Research has shown that the word *mama* is the first word that most babies utter. Research has also shown that babies' first words have to do with one of three categories: animals, food, and toys. Action words such as *eat* are among the first to appear. These action words first describe only the baby's action; later, the same word may be used to described someone else's actions. Bear in mind that the *sequence* of events is the important thing; variations in the *age* at which these milestones appear are completely normal.

» For the first six months or so your contribution to language development should consist primarily of exchanges of simple expressions and your own simple phrases as you interact with the baby. Be sure to take turns in your "conversations" with your baby. Even at six weeks or so, when you are playing your communicating game, you should take turns. The dialogue may start with a smile as you look into her eyes and say a few words. Wait. Give her a chance to react. This waiting time is essential; the gap establishes a chance for the baby to participate. You may only get a stare, perhaps a smile or a cooing sound. Now it's your turn. The idea is to offer an occasion for turn-taking. Here are a few suggestions for such interaction:

- When you pick up, roll over, or feed the baby, use descriptive words to characterize the way things might feel to the baby. (It should go without saying that using baby's name often is an excellent idea at this stage and, indeed, during the other five as well.)

- Point out variations in temperatures, textures, etc.

- Give the baby plenty of opportunities to be near adults and children as they talk. Listening to human speech is a natural and necessary process to the acquisition of language.

During the second six months, you can expand on your repertoire of activities and games in the language-development area. Toy telephones, games that require naming body parts, labels of objects with which the child comes in daily contact, and walks designed for pointing out, touching, and seeing different things are all excellent activities.

(Later in the book, we will discuss language development following the first year of life.)

MOVING ON

Stage I babies are capable of surviving and flourishing in a loving, nurturing human environment, even though they are restricted to a few reflexes and primitive perceptions.

Please remember that a stage is noticeable by the appearance and persistence of certain specific attainments and limitations. An age boundary is placed around stages because that is generally when these specific attainments and limitations manifest themselves. But these age notations should not be thought of as definitive pronouncements of when their corresponding behaviors appear. They are general guidelines.

> **Age does not determine stage—it is only an approximation of when a given action is expected.**

All of my suggestions for this stage and the ones that follow are based on certain fundamental understandings: that the joy of parenting starts with an attitude and atmosphere of relaxed warmth, love and caring; that activities should be enjoyed in a spirit of fun and guided play, when baby is attentive and in a calm, relaxed state; and that respect for baby's comfort and safety should never be overlooked.

SUMMARY OF INTELLECTUAL ATTAINMENTS
(STAGE I: Birth to one month)

Intellectual Activity

Focuses at a distance of about eight inches.

Prefers to look at human faces, contours, and contrasts.

Enjoys sounds, prefers high-pitched voices, soft music.

Grasps objects firmly.

Looks at people for brief periods.

Falls asleep if overstimulated.

Turns face in the direction of object touching cheeks.

Sucks at objects touching mouth area.

Responds to touch.

Vocalizes, as in crying, cooing, babbling.

◆

CHAPTER SIX

Stage II
(1 to 4 Months)
Body-Oriented Learning

When your baby was in her first month of life (Stage I), her knowledge system was limited to objects or situations that triggered simple survival reflex actions. These were independent actions, with no connection to each other. Exercising reflex actions helped refine them.

Now that Nancy is one month old, you will notice separate reflex actions beginning to be coordinated and organized, while new action patterns become more elaborate, more "wholistic." Stage II ushers in the possibility of acquiring new patterns of behavior as a result of interaction with the environment. Nancy has a newly developed ability to learn and acquire her first habits. This is body-oriented learning.

» While sucking was reflexive and served only a nourishing function during Stage I, in Stage II Nancy sucks not only for nourishment, but for pleasure and exploration as well. She learns to suck her thumb, thereby differentiating the need (hunger) from the act (sucking). The ability to coordinate one action with another opens up a magnificent new world of learning.

Stage II brings us to the heart of *all* learning: the continuous process of differentiation and integration and the resulting possibility of accommodation. We humans adjust to the world revealed to us through knowledge and experience. We begin to do so at this stage.

Stage II babies can, for instance, learn to change their grasp of an object according to its shape or to adjust their posture according to the way they are held. These apparently small accommodations are in fact the signposts of profound mental growth; they represent intelligent adaptations to one's surroundings. Without this process, human learning would be impossible.

PRIMARY CIRCULAR REACTIONS

This Piaget phrase is best explained by example: Quite by chance, Samuel brings his hand by his face and suddenly finds his thumb in his mouth. This event is called primary, because it involves the baby's own body. Samuel repeats the action over and over again until it is well learned and becomes habitual—or circular, because it is repeated.

Primary circular reactions show that an infant can extend reflex actions into semi-intentional acts, a profound accomplishment that represents a major advance from the reacting newborn. Your baby is now able to imitate action and, to some extent, control his environment. To accomplish the thumb-sucking feat, Samuel had to differentiate his hand (thumb) from his mouth. He now looks at his hand as a separate object. And even though he invented the action quite by accident, he can repeat it.

Your contribution is to help Samuel find his hand again by removing distracting objects. In general, you should be aware of the importance of repetitive actions involving Samuel's own body and encourage them.

REFINEMENTS (WITH A PURPOSE)

In his first month of life we saw the baby busily refining his innately given reflexes and primitive perceptions. By practicing his reflex actions and his perceptual skills, baby Scott improved his physical skills. Refinements involving the mouth, hands, eyes, legs, and body are the main focus at this point. The second stage sees Scott performing these skills with even greater refinement. The difference is now that he combines his well-practiced skills *to accomplish some practical goal.*

Mouth. Try a few games to encourage refinements related to the mouth area.

- Can your baby discriminate between certain tastes and temperatures of liquids? Does drooling change when he is given sugar water, milk, juice, or cold/warm water?

» Expose your baby to a variety of textured objects. Let him handle and mouth them. Be sure they are nontoxic and safe. Don't overwhelm your infant; present only one new object at a time. Some suggestions: wooden spoons, wooden rings, plastic balls, terrycloth, velvet, silk-like material, rubber, foam, crumpled paper.

Hands. Even now, Scott enjoys grasping onto your finger when you place it in his palm. Provide opportunities for exercising this action.

- Place your finger in the palm of his hand and watch him grasp it. Then gently pull away. Repeat this activity a few times.

« Hand your baby objects of different sizes, shapes and textures. Try terrycloth, silk, hard/soft balls, blocks, straws, and paper. Brush his fingers with the objects. How long will he hold it? Can the object just touch the tips of his fingers in order to bring about grasping?

When the baby's hands respond to even the slightest touch, this is a sign of progress. By the end of Stage II, grasping will become completely voluntary. Now is a good time to introduce easy-to-hold rattles, rings, and other safe objects.

Rattles are wonderful: shaken, they make a sound, thereby allowing babies to experience competence. In controlling aspects of their environment, babies feel a sense of mastery. This is important not only in terms of their intellectual development, but for their self-concept as well. The feedback from the toy helps baby to adjust her actions and improve her manner of grasping, shaking, manipulating, examining, listening, mouthing, and so on.

Here are some good commercially produced rattles:

- *Ring Rattle by Kiddercraft.*
- *Key Rattle Teether by Kiddercraft.*
- *Rattle from Johnson and Johnson Child Development Series.*

Eyes. While Baby Scott is also developing his perceptual powers at this stage, he still prefers to look at contours, patterns, and contrasts. Accordingly, it still makes sense to emphasize these features—as opposed to color, size, or brightness—in his bedding, crib accessories, and toys. The crib bumper we started with (the black and white one with the human faces) will continue to do just fine.

- Since he enjoys looking at faces, your face is better than any! Look baby in the eye; smile; talk to him; occasionally, make a point of moving from top to bottom and from side to side as you play with him, change him, and follow your daily routine.
- A round throw pillow with a human face crochet would be a nice addition to the crib now. Some boldly striped pillows would be great, too.
- Give your baby stuffed animals or dolls with large faces.
- Change the mobile when your baby's interest seems to wane. Attach brightly colored pieces of paper, cloth, clothespins, small bells, and/or large rings to varying lengths of elastic. You might use bright, shiny foil to make a mobile that will reflect light from a window. This will aid in development of eye muscle coordination. Use your imagination! Make sure that the mobile is completely safe: it should be high enough so that your baby cannot get tangled in it and made of non-toxic materials.

» Move a rattle from one side of the baby's body to the other, and from top to bottom. Gently shake it as you bring it slowly in a half circle from the center to the baby's left side, back to the center, and then to the right.

- In a darkened room, use a flashlight to bounce light right and left, up and down. Your baby will soon follow the light with his eyes.

Babies enjoy looking at large moving objects. (Any parent who has taken an infant to a restaurant with a ceiling fan can attest to this!) A new mobile or a rod and frame device hung over his crib will both be great fun to watch. If you walk as you hold him so you can both watch people and pets coming and going around the house, you will produce the same enjoyable effect. Interacting with others (new faces!) is also fun for him: encourage new contacts, such as those with older brothers or sisters. But make an effort to be close by when the baby encounters others. New people may be frightening.

During this stage, the baby will refine her perceptions to the point where she can recognize you, her caretaker, and become aware of herself as separate from other objects and people.

She is becoming aware of herself; she has discovered a new reality. As we have seen, any new discovery needs to be practiced. So allow baby to touch her face, feet, eyes, and mouth as you play with her, bathe her, and so on. You can help by holding her hands and bringing them to her cheeks, head, nose, and other parts of her body.

 « Try tying a small, colorful ribbon or bracelet made of yarn around the baby's wrist. This may draw attention to this part of the body. Another variation: place a colorful sock mitten or even a small brightly colored sticker on the baby's hand.

ACCOMMODATING

We have seen that as early as the first month baby can adjust his body to the way you are holding him. No longer the helpless newborn, the Stage II baby can change himself to fit the demands of the situation to some extent—he can *accommodate!*

> **There will be many attempts at accommodation now, and our objectives in Stage II are to be aware of these attempts and to support them.**

Notice that the baby can now sit and stand briefly while being supported: this is not the "walking reflex" of the newborn, but a new and exciting skill that requires practice. Help the baby sit and stand up while you support him; he will enjoy working on his new-found abilities.

» Your baby will enjoy being held upright for ten to fifteen minutes. Don't overdo it, though.

Take a shiny foreign object like an aluminum pie pan and hold it at arm's length from your baby. Allow him time to adjust to the new object before bringing it closer. See how your baby reacts to new "ideas." This activity aids in the the baby's ability to incorporate novel objects into his "world."

COORDINATIONS

What are the most important examples of coordination at this period? Actually, there are only a few coordinated actions that you need to be aware of. We've already looked at one in some detail: thumb-sucking, part of the coordinated movement of arms and mouth.

At this stage, thumb-sucking is a very common, independent activity. Besides occasionally repositioning the baby's hand by her side after a chance contact, there is little you can do to enhance this coordination. (And there is certainly no need to try to restrict the activity now.)

In playing with baby, you can help her with her new coordination.

- While she is on her back, hold her wrists with your hands and help her with a patty-cake game. Finish the game by moving her hands up to her cheeks so she can explore them. On occasion, bring her hands up to your cheeks instead.

What else is new at Stage II? Eye coordination is making major strides. Upon waking, before she starts to cry, whether lying down or propped up to sitting, baby may stare at objects dangling overhead, turn her head to follow something moving, and even smile at moving objects or people. You will occasionally see the start of expressed interest in her hands and feet.

In addition to the mobiles and variety shows we have discussed, you may now want to use sound-producing toys or toys that feature bouncing movements. All will help stimulate eye coordination.

» During the latter portion of Stage II, you can introduce the mirror. Not only is it fun to gaze at, but it will help her differentiate herself as an independent object in this world. Gradually she will develop a concept of self quite distinct from other things out there. Nancy will occasionally pound at her image in the mirror. Initially, it may startle her. Then she'll repeat this action again and again.

You will begin to notice that your baby is turning her head in the direction of sound. This action involves a slightly different coordination than that of eye movements and hearing. The baby will often interrupt her own activity and look attentively in the direction of the sound. Of course, some sounds are more pleasurable than others. Regardless, sounds and sound-producing things are now of great interest to her.

 Once you notice your baby turning toward the direction of a sound, you can do a great deal to nurture this new development.

SOUND GAMES

- Try repeating the earlier activity of moving an object from side to side, but this time use a little bell, or simply snap your fingers as you move a puppet.

- Make clicking sounds as you face baby while she is on her back, moving your face from side to side. You can also sing, hum, and talk to her as you change her and care for her.

- Dangle sound-producing toys, such as little squeaker balls, in front of the baby. Swing the toys gently.

- Hang chimes near a window so the baby hears soft music each time the wind blows through the room.

- Play different kinds of music; see what your baby seems to prefer.

- Expose your infant to a variety of household sounds—vacuum cleaner, doorbells, barking dogs. Provide all sorts of listening stimulation.

- When the baby is on her stomach, hold a rattle directly in front of her face. Slowly lift the rattle so that the baby follows the noise by raising her head. Encourage her, if necessary, by gently pushing her up on her hands. Lower the object and, as always, repeat.

VOCAL IMITATION

The infant in Stage II begins to imitate his own utterances and behavior as well as that of others. This important advance means that the baby can remember an event at least long enough to be able to reproduce it.

Little wails may precede crying and are kept up for their own sake. Cooing and gurgling follow. This is the point at which Tommy practices vocalizations over and over again, often stopping in surprise then starting the cycle again. Frequently, you may conclude that the *only* reason he keeps crying is to hear himself vocalize!

» *He is beginning to learn for the very first time.*

» *He is beginning to imitate himself.*

» *He can coordinate his actions and produce a repeatable action.*

» *He repeats the action often enough to develop a habit.*

These traits herald the beginning of a memory of actions and a sense of physical causality.

If you play a musical instrument, you probably know exactly what I mean by a memory of actions. In playing my guitar, I often try to recollect some part of a piece and mentally reconstruct how it is played, to no avail. But if I start to play the preceding segment of that piece, the rest of it "just comes to me." Most people can recall similar experiences. We all know that once you learn how to ride a bicycle, you always know how. Your baby's "motor memory" is now taking shape. Simple imagery is also developing, which is the reason your baby can recognize you.

You can nurture this natural tendency in many ways.

- Reproduce your baby's utterances. Wait for her to produce another sound and then repeat the process. This "communication" exercise encourages baby to vocalize. Once in a while you can change the sound or the emphasis, tone, or number of repetitions of the utterance. Your baby may even imitate what you do!

You will find that your baby's vocal activity will increase in reaction to the sounds made by others. How can you encourage this ability?

« When you hear your baby making a sound, such as "ah," you can then say a prolonged "aaaah." Soon baby will, in turn, imitate you.

This form of imitation is limited, of course, to sounds that the baby knows how produce. This is another example of your baby's ability to coordinate events—integrating hearing with vocalizing. Listening to his own voice and vocalizations will often stimulate additional vocalizations. Babies really do enjoy hearing themselves!

- Nod your head back and forth and up and down as you speak to your baby. Does your baby try to follow your actions? If he waits until you have stopped before beginning nodding, this shows accommodation. He is studying your moves first and modifying his actions to fit yours.

- Sing a musical scale. Does your baby's intonation follow your own?

NEW WAYS OF KNOWING

As infants develop their intelligence, they gradually construct more elaborate and stable understandings of the reality of their surroundings, a reality founded on their understanding of objects, time, space, and causality. For example, a baby's understanding of an object, say a rattle, evolves over time and experience. In the first month of life the rattle was not a distinct separate object. Now it is.

Compare your knowledge of the rattle with that of your baby. Obviously, your understanding of the rattle is much deeper. You know its physical features, its attributes, and how these relate to other objects. You know its price and its function. You also know that just because the rattle falls on the floor out of your sight, that does not mean it has vanished from the face of the earth. In contrast, the baby knows that this thing is something to shake, bang, and put in the mouth. That is all.

As the baby interacts with the rattle, he realizes that it can be moved (in *space*), and that this moving happens in *time* (there is a sequence to it—first he grasps it, then shakes it, then bangs it, then puts it in his mouth). Shaking it *causes* a rattling sound—that's the beginning of understanding physical causality, or what causes something to happen.

> When a child interacts with an object, he constructs two things: know-how (the methods of his own abilities) and knowledge of the object itself.

Remember, all thought stems from action. First one knows on a working, actional plane. Then and only then one can internalize or represent that knowledge through a symbolic system to know on a thoughtful level.

Bearing this in mind, let's look again at the Stage II baby's capabilities with respect to the categories of knowledge. Contrary to Stage I (when the infant had absolutely no notion of the concept of object), Stage II infant development includes coordination of a number of abilities and events, giving a sense of stability. As we have seen, the baby learns in this stage to relate a sound to its source. Repetition of this relation emphasizes the existence of something real, creating a readiness for the object concept, although a very premature one.

Another significant step being taken by the Stage II infant is the predecessor of the understanding that an object does have an existence all its own: the baby looks at the spot where visual contact with the object was lost. Let's say you move a rattle in front of your baby and she follows it with her eyes. If, at a certain point, you cover the rattle with your hand, the baby will continue to look at your hand for a short time. She does not look for long; nor does she visually search for the rattle. But she does watch briefly for the object to reappear.

Now, we have seen that active searching for vanished objects is the first real indication that babies have constructed an understanding of the permanence of objects. The Stage II baby does not give us that indication; she shows a kind of passive expectation, expecting the object to be where she last saw it.

> **The Stage II baby has not yet taken the next step, which is to actively search for the object visually. As for her concepts of space, time, and causality, similar "small steps" are the order of the day.**

Full understanding—even on an exclusively active plane—is yet to come.

The following chart summarizes the attainments of the Stage II baby, and provides an *approximate* chronological look at important attainments during this stage. *Please view it solely as a guideline for the appearance of abilities and remember that the age range for the appearance of a given attainment is only a rough estimate.* Children differ widely in the rate at which they develop, so don't be concerned if your baby does not adhere strictly to these broad standards.

The important point to remember is that the Stage I baby is qualitatively different from the Stage II baby.

Whereas the Stage I baby's actions are reflexive, the Stage II baby has outgrown this reflexive nature of knowing and has developed the capability of learning simple actions and coordinations involving his own body.

SUMMARY OF INTELLECTUAL ATTAINMENTS
(STAGE II: One to four months)

Intellectual Activity

END OF FIRST MONTH

Prefers contours, patterns, and contrasts.

Reflexes become more refined.

Turns head to orient in the direction of sound.

Looks attentively at adult.

Adjusts body to way being held.

END OF SECOND MONTH

Stares at large, moving, contoured objects.

Responds to people and prefers them to other objects.

Primary circular reaction
(repeats actions involving own body).

Looks at her hand as an object:

Associates two contiguous events
(e.g., mother's voice with eating).

Eye movements continue to improve.

END OF THIRD MONTH / BEGINNING OF FOURTH MONTH

Grasping becomes voluntary.

Establishes hand-eye coordination.

Becomes aware of self.

Orients in the direction of sound.

Produces sounds and imitates own sounds.

Can sit and stand briefly while supported.

Recognizes caretaker.

Swings at objects.

Age approximations are intended as guidelines only. Please regard them as rough estimates.

CHAPTER SEVEN

◆

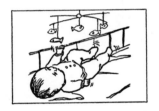

Stage III
(4 to 8 Months)
Externally-Oriented Actions

◆

AS THE BABY ENTERS STAGE III, development has progressed beyond body-oriented learning. Now your baby's actions involve the outside world, and so does her learning.

» Nicole's physical development has progressed to include crawling and all that it entails: exploration, discovery, and manipulation of the physical world. Her physical mobility, along with her newly developed ability to coordinate various senses with motoric activity, means she is now quite literally ready to reach out to the wondrous world of objects all around her.

 The Stage III baby is distinguished by her ability to exercise skills to manipulate the external world of objects. The objective at this stage is to provide as many opportunities as possible for the development of those skills.

Baby's improved hand-eye coordination permits her to extend her horizon and grasp things she finds within her reach. You might provide easy-to-manipulate objects, such as rattles, rings, wooden spoons, plastic measuring cups, large plastic canisters and their covers, and so on.

Not surprisingly, one of our first priorities at this stage is to provide a safe space for crawling. Safety throughout the house now becomes a very important area of attention. Open stairs, low cabinets, and small objects left lying around are some of the potential hazards to guard against. Store all household chemicals and cleaners, drugs, and other potentially harmful substances and objects out of the baby's reach. Turn the water heater thermostat down so as to prevent accidental scalding; plug in or block all unused electrical outlets.

SECONDARY CIRCULAR REACTIONS

« Christopher is lying on his back in his crib, happily watching his toes as he moves his legs around. Suddenly, he notices that the mobile suspended above his crib is moving. In an effort to reproduce the turning of the mobile he thrashes his legs around again. As he succeeds in activating the mobile, he'll repeat the process over and over again. How he enjoys repeating the newly learned pattern!

A frequently repeated action directed toward an object outside the infant's body is known as a secondary circular reaction—secondary, because it involves objects beyond the baby's body; circular, because it is repeated again and again.

 When you see evidence of secondary circular reactions, you can be sure that your baby has entered Stage III.

Four steps are identified with secondary circular reactions.

1. Baby accidentally produces an interesting outcome.
2. Baby perceives a connection between his act and the external outcome.
3. Baby repeats the process.
4. Baby learns to perform an action that consistently reproduces events.

Here are some ideas on how to interact meaningfully with your baby in play.

» Dangle bells, chimes, rattles, cloth balls, etc. from baby's crib to increase the chances of his accidentally producing an effect that he can then reproduce on purpose.

» Use a kick board that has bells attached to it.

« Buy a kicking mobile and attach it to baby's play pen.

« With ribbon, not string, gently tie a balloon to baby's ankle and watch him discover the connection between his actions and the balloon's behavior.

« Tie a balloon, bell, or ball of yarn to a wrist band. If you wish to buy one, I recommend the Wrist Rattle by Fisher-Price.

« Give your baby a small piece of cloth with bells sewn on. When he shakes the cloth or picks it up, the bells ring.

« Hang objects by pieces of elastic above the crib or playpen. Try to use objects that will produce a noise when your baby hits them.

» Attach a toy to a string and place the string in the baby's hand. Use a variety of toys: a tambourine, a bell, noise makers, and squeakers, as well as silent objects.

» In the bathtub, encourage your baby to splash around. He may realize that his motions cause ripples in the water.

» A baby jump seat, one which uses your baby's bouncing and jumping to propel him forward, helps with the causality concept. Your baby's actions accidentally cause a very interesting result: his own movement! This activity also allows your baby to move through space to get to objects, thus enhancing the space/distance concept.

» Supply your baby with a wooden spoon and a pot. He will discover that hitting the pot with the spoon produces an exciting new noise. Give your baby different pots, pans, and other objects that produce varying noises when hit.

When baby perceives a relationship between his act and the resulting event, he is forming a primitive notion of cause and effect, or causality. To reproduce an event, he must construct a practical understanding of means-ends. In other words, he must know that doing this produces that. This brings us to the subject of intentionality, the issue of "meaning" to do a certain thing.

SEMI-INTENTIONAL ACTIONS

Can we speak, at this stage, of intention on the part of a baby?

> Nicole thrashes around and notices that the mobile above her crib turns. Later, she repeats the actions to produce the same result. Are her actions intentional?

Is Nicole's "meaning" to turn her mobile similar in any way to your intention to, say, drive into town once you get in your car in the morning? The answer is yes: a form of intentionality must certainly be present. She tried to repeat actions that produced interesting outcomes. The intention in question is *not* fully developed, however, because the baby first only caused the mobile to turn accidentally. Had she thought of the goal first, then initiated the action to realize it, the act would have been fully intentional.

« Secondary circular reactions, such as the repetition of the motion necessary to make water splash agreeably—and, at first, surprisingly—in the bathtub, are limited in nature. They reproduce events that were brought about quite by chance. They cannot be fully intentional, because they are not invented by the baby.

Such actions, far from being inventive, are repetitions of efforts the baby is already capable of doing. We can describe these actions as semi-intentional. By the end of

Stage III, Nicole will see herself as a means to various ends. She will know that she can cause things to happen, and derive tremendous pleasure from practicing her new, steadily growing mental powers.

This is a good time to play with toys that you and baby can have some predictable influence on.

» Pull a toy to draw it nearer to you and baby.

» Roll a ball back and forth.

» Pull a string to ring a bell.

» Shake the crib rail to make the mobile turn.

You can also turn these semi-intentional action games into occasions for social play:

« Puff up your cheeks and, taking baby's hands, bring them against your cheeks to let the air out. Repeat.

« Bring baby's hands to your mouth while you make a babbling sound. Repeat.

Children are absolutely delighted with this kind of play. No matter which game you play, make sure that you repeat the same pattern over and over again. Incidentally, baby will tell you when you are overdoing it—she will turn the game off by refusing to focus on it!

This is also a good time to reinstate your vocal imitation games as the baby continues to imitate sounds he had produced before. Watch for baby's vocalizations and his own imitations of them. Then join in the fun by imitating the vocalizations and by varying them slightly to see if he follows your lead.

« Hands are the key elements in Stage III development. Your baby can now grasp and release an object at will. He shows great interest in grasping and, increasingly, manipulating objects and events in the outside world. He has greater control over hand movements and much better hand-eye coordination.

In Stage II, baby explored things mainly with his eyes. In Stage III, it is his hands that do the exploring, and they are everywhere: touching, holding, manipulating.

Many of the activities that you were doing with your baby in Stages I and II are still quite appropriate in Stage III. However, all the fragile mobiles and "swallowable" objects of the early stages must now be removed and replaced with sturdier, larger ones and things with smooth, safe surfaces. Items that are securely fastened to the crib can remain.

Since he can reach for things, be sure to dangle or offer only completely safe objects within his reach. These may be objects suspended with a ribbon, mobiles (again), and hanging cradle gyms.

» Help baby crawl. Place her in jumper seats to discover how her actions can result in an outcome.

» A push and pop toy or a colorful pinwheel will introduce the baby to new sounds and movements.

Purchase a funhouse activity center; they can offer many hours of fun and learning experiences. There are a number of these on the market. Ambi manufactures an excellent Funhouse, as do Kiddercraft and Fisher-Price. You might also look at busy boxes designed for water play to use at bath time. Some of them contain wheels that turn as water is poured into them. Show baby how this is done; help him try to do it himself.

A word about playthings, which now take on greater importance than ever. Toys should be easy to grasp from any angle and should be "graspable" with one hand. Edges on toys should be round and smooth. Be sure there are no detachable parts. Check labels for any harmful materials or dyes used in the manufacturing process. Since almost everything ends up in baby's mouth, it's a good idea to wash things before play time. And since Stage III is a very active stage, filled with dropping, banging, squeezing, pinching, and chewing, it is wise to keep durability in mind when toy shopping.

The baby likes to relate the new learning to what is already known and use it as it was used before. As you play with the Stage III baby, be prepared to see some "old favorites" take a few surprising turns.

« Rolling a ball or pulling a familiar toy in front of your baby may result in a fascinated reappraisal of the object. Allow him to pick up small objects with his fingers; this stimulates small hand muscles and eye-hand coordination.

« He now gets a great deal of pleasure from taking things apart. Playing with a set of small pots and pans is a great source of learning and fun. Put one pot inside another, then separate them. But don't be surprised if he can't put them back together. That will come later.

» Babies begin to distinguish colors between the ages of six and twelve months.
Use your felt banner (mentioned in the
chapter on Stage I) to introduce brightly
colored pictures and shapes. Talk to your
baby as you point out the different colors.
Emphasize colors in all of your daily activities: choose pretty colored towels for
bathing, solid colored toys and objects,
colored plastic flatware, etc.

Earlier, your baby displayed an interest in his hands.
Now help him to discover his feet as well.

» With your baby lying on his back,
brush his toes with a rattle few times.
Does he extend his leg and kick? Raise
the rattle higher, sweep to the right and
then to the left. Can he coordinate his
actions to move his feet closer to the
rattle? Note that his understanding of
his hands does not always extend to
his feet.

» Present a toy that is actually old but
appears new. You might, for instance,
attach a bell to a rubber duck. Normally
your baby produces a "bell noise" by
shaking the bell and a "duck noise" by
squeezing. What is his reaction to producing a noise by shaking the duck?

» Pull and stretch games are very good
at this age. Connect two cloth balls with
a piece of elastic. Hold one end and encourage the baby to hold the other.
Stretch the elastic and release.

« Explore textures. Give your baby a few
hard things at a time, then some soft,
then some fuzzy objects. Talk to him about
it. Your words are not for the sake of
teaching language but for teaching
that words are used to name things.

THE OBJECT CONCEPT STRENGTHENS

Early in Stage III, if you drop a rattle in front of your
baby, chances are she won't follow it. But later in this
stage (at approximately seven months), if she sees the
start of the rattle's fall, she will look around on the blanket in front of her to find it.

This searching for a vanished object marks the continuing progression of the object concept. The baby
might drop keys, a rattle, or a plastic ring and then visually search for it. Furthermore, if she spots part of an
object, she understands that the rest of it is hidden and
yes, she will definitely want to find it. Conversely, if she
doesn't see any part of the object, she will abandon the
visual search.

Your baby goes through several steps in understanding that objects have permanence. In Stage II, we saw
that the baby demonstrated no visual search for vanished objects. The Stage III baby does show visual
search. And the Stage IV baby shows manual search for
a disappearing object.

The baby's memory has evolved, too. He can now distinguish between old things and new ones. You might
keep some old toys even though you are introducing

new ones, though once baby no longer shows any interest in a toy, you may wish to give it away.

These are gradual developments: images coming steadily into focus, not switches being flicked on in an instant. The distinct attainments at each stage, however, offer an idea of some of the structural features of the remarkable growth patterns in force at this moment within your child's mind.

PEOPLE LEARNING

During Stage III, social interaction profoundly stimulates a baby's intellect.

> Secure a nonbreakable mirror to the crib bumper so baby can respond to herself and further her own separate identity. It is also fun to stand with baby in your arms in front of a wall mirror so that she can see both your faces.

But the greatest wonder and delight are brought out by the game of peek-a-boo.

Playing a variety of peek-a-boo games provides an excellent opportunity for your child to exercise his understanding of the concept of permanence of objects. For the four-to-eight-month-old, the experience seems magical. How can something disappear (that, is, cease to exist!) only to appear again?

Peek-a-boo games in which your baby can see a part of you (while the other part is hiding) confirm his newly established expectations that the rest of you can be found. You will find that the baby's instinct is to play the game over and over again; do not deny him. Enjoy the thrill that the baby is experiencing.

It is certainly worth reviewing a variety of peek-a-boo games here because they do so much for development and are so much fun for the baby.

« In the initial phases of Stage III, play peek-a-boo games in which you hide your face, revealing a small portion of it.

« Later, play the game by hiding a toy behind an object, partially revealing a portion of it.

« Since baby will visually follow a falling object to its resting position, show her a small, light, plastic bell and drop it in front of baby on his blanket. Repeat this and watch baby's eyes to see if he is anticipating the fall to its resting position.

« Still later in Stage III the baby will visually search for a vanished object. Hide objects, such as a set of plastic keys, behind a pillow. Draw baby's attention to the keys and when he focuses on it, cover them with a blanket. Uncover while baby is still watching.

» By the end of this period baby searches for an object that was grasped by continuing the same gripping movement. Slip a toy out of baby's hand. Watch for the grasping movements, then place it back in baby's hand.

A number of commercially produced peek-a-boo toys are available. Here are the best.

- Peek-a-Boo Bunny by Kiddercraft. This toy combines reaching, grasping, and pulling to effect the peek-a-boo action by the toy bunny.
- A crib peek-a-boo that combines reaching, grasping, and pulling to hide faces behind a "board" is Toy Mount Peek-a-Boo by Semper/Fischerform.
- A unique variation on the jack-in-the-box is Jack-in-the-Ball by Ambi.

SPATIAL RELATIONS

Stage III affords you an opportunity to expand on the child's spatial concepts, as well. Here are some suggestions.

» Instead of simply placing objects in your baby's hands each time, try bringing the object slowly within reach. How close must the object be before he'll reach for it? Does the distance vary depending on the size of the object?

« Move a rattle so that the baby must reach first in front of him, then to the right, then to the left, then up in the air. This is to encourage reaching.

« Supply your baby with a spoon, a toothbrush and a comb, and then dangle a baby shoe in front of him by its lace. Allow the baby to discover how the varying intensity of his swings affects the object when it is hit.

« While looking in the mirror, show your baby the reflection of a toy. Then move it behind him, still keeping the toy visible in the mirror. Where does he reach? He can see the toy in the mirror but not behind him!

DURING STAGE III . . .

- Baby stumbles upon reactions accidentally and repeats them in an effort to make interesting environmental outcomes last.
- Baby begins to manipulate the external world.
- Early crawling activity may take place.

It is worth repeating that the age at which children attain and master any process varies. Let your natural instincts and your knowledge of your own baby determine how you can use suggestions for enriching activities.

Enjoy the fun that comes with thinking up activities for your child's intellectual enhancement.

SUMMARY OF INTELLECTUAL ATTAINMENTS
(STAGE III: Four to eight months)

Intellectual Activity

END OF FOURTH MONTH

Reproduces an environmental outcome originally produced by chance.

Begins to crawl and manipulate objects.

Recognizes relationship between acts and outcomes.

Repeats newly learned behavior patterns.

Distinguishes new from old toys.

Continues to imitate sounds he had produced before.

END OF FIFTH MONTH

Reaches for object.

Anticipates entire object by seeing only part of it.

END OF SIXTH MONTH

Interested in containers.

Visually anticipates position of falling object.

Visually searches for vanished object.

END OF SEVENTH MONTH / BEGINNING OF EIGHTH MONTH

Reaches for, grasps, manipulates and mouths objects.

Responds to mirror image.

Searches for object that was grasped and lost from grip by continuing same movements.

Age approximations to be regarded strictly as guidelines. Please consider these as rough estimates only.

CHAPTER EIGHT

Stage IV
(8 to 12 Months)
Means and Ends

As WE HAVE SEEN, infant growth is a subtle, incremental thing. However gradual change may be, though, virtually every parent has an experience of sudden awe and wonder in considering the accomplishments that have accumulated by the time the baby reaches the fourth stage of intellectual growth. A few months ago, your child was an essentially passive and reflex-dependent being. How much has changed!

The Stage III baby is distinguished by her enormous and rapid learning. Stage IV is a time for consolidating and reconciling the attainments of the past and extending them to apply to new and different situations. This is an exciting time for the baby and for you as well.

As we preview the special mental attainments of this next stage, remember that they have their roots in Stage III and are outgrowths of skills developed earlier. Stages don't proceed along a linear dimension or disappear to be replaced with new ones. New patterns and new ways of adapting to the world arise when one previous stage merges into the next.

Piaget characterized Stage IV by its *deferred circular reactions*. By this he meant repetitive reactions (the secondary circular reactions we learned about earlier) that the baby can stop in order to pay attention to another event, then reinstate.

Deferred circular reactions reflect the ability to interrupt reactions, defer them to a later time, and then pick them up again.

This ability suggests the baby now has a memory system capable of storing and retrieving his own actions.

THE DAWN OF FULL INTENT . . . AND OTHER MILESTONES

In this stage, several major attainments are being perfected, including the concept of means-ends relations. Now an infant shows an intentional selection of means to accomplish preestablished goals. Your baby shows clear signs of elementary planning. You may see him, for instance, move one object out of his way to get another.

In Stage III baby could visually search for a vanished object. Now he begins to search for a vanished object manually! This is an extremely important development; it illustrates the enhancement of the understanding that objects that go out of sight do not necessarily disappear altogether.

Imitation has progressed to the point where baby can reproduce an action involving parts of her body she cannot see. This is crucial because it allows her to accommodate herself to new situation. Such adjustments are a further sign of adaptability or flexibility, which we identified earlier as the essence of all intelligence.

Another area of progress is that of *anticipation*. The baby associates certain events to other preceding events. When a sequence is disrupted, she shows surprise.

Finally, the Stage IV baby has grown to understand that not only can she be the source of activity, but other objects and other people can also cause things to happen. This insight is fundamental for a full understanding of cause-effect relations. It is your baby's first step toward scientific learning!

As the baby puts these forms of intelligent actions to work, he builds his knowledge of reality. He knows that the hidden object he wishes to see again exists somewhere, and he searches for it with his hands near where it was last seen. Baby has also developed his concepts of *space* and *time* more fully, understanding on a practical level such concepts as "in," "out," "behind," "through," etc. These remarkable aptitudes all work together to bring him a richer and fuller understanding of the world than he has ever known.

Let's take a closer look at each of the prominent Stage IV abilities.

MEANS-ENDS RELATIONS

Adults tend to take the notion of means and ends—the idea, for instance, that turning on the television set will result in a picture—more or less for granted. For your baby, such patterns of implicit relationships between events are only beginning to emerge. Previously her world has been characterized for the most part by a series of seemingly random and unconnected events. Now, in Stage IV, your baby is confirming her recent suspicion that there is more to this series of surprises than meets the eye. And she is beginning to use that confirmation to her advantage.

> **Our first concrete clue that a baby has entered Stage IV occurs when she demonstrates the ability to select a means intentionally in order to attain a preestablished goal.**

In one illustration of this development, Piaget described how he showed an object to his son Laurent but placed his hands in front of it as an obstacle, leaving the object only partially in view. At seven months, seventeen days, Laurent tried to get the object by hitting his father's hand, while at nine months, fifteen days, he pushed his father's hand away with one hand while grabbing the object with the other. Laurent's second action was *intentional* in that he separated the means from the end.

This story illustrates the Stage IV baby's ability to invent new coordination. Laurent organized his prior learning in such a way as to conceive of the means (pushing Daddy's hand away) before reaching the goal (getting the object). This ability is what separates the Stage IV baby from her previous ways of knowing. You can safely assume that your Stage IV baby will, from this point forward, strive eagerly to conceive of new ways to reach a goal. In fact, most parents are probably well advised to enjoy this resourcefulness while it operates on a comparatively small scale. In a year or so, you will be both amazed and exhausted at the apparently limitless resolve your child will show in attempting to attain her goals!

HOW DO YOU KNOW YOUR BABY'S ACTIONS ARE INTENTIONAL?

The answer is simple: experiment.

» Try this. With your baby focused on what you're doing, throw a set of keys in front of him. His first reaction will be to reach for the keys and mouth them. Now throw the keys behind another object (say a pillow). What will he do? One of two things: show his anger and frustration, and cry, or reach out toward the pillow, then push it away to expose the keys so he can grab them.

If he cries in frustration, he simply has a little more developing to do. But if he pushes the pillow to get the keys, he is showing—with great authority—that he has already developed a capacity for intentional action. Solving such problems requiring elementary planning is a clear example of Stage IV behavior.

By the way, don't be alarmed if your eight-month-old doesn't solve this problem. Remember, we are not in a race. Children are not replicas of some ideal model you will find delineated in the pages of this or any other book. They are all different, and their intellectual development will vary somewhat. Minor variations from the norm are nothing to fret over.

The solution of the missing-object problem, when it does occur, illustrates the remarkable ability of a Stage IV baby to construct a mental bridge of sorts in order to pass over a recognized obstacle. You can be sure your baby's actions are intentional when ...

> ... he uses an indirect approach to reach a goal when some obstacle prevents him from achieving it.

> ... he doesn't stumble accidentally upon the goal while playing but shows signs he conceived of the goal before he initiated the action to attain it.

> ... he overcomes the obstacle by different means from the ones he normally uses to reach his goal.

Our example of the keys passes all three tests. Baby attempted to get the keys directly by reaching for them but was prevented from doing so by the obstacle. He had to think of pushing away the pillow to get the keys. Finally, he figured out a new way to get the keys.

 « Here is another experiment. You show your child a rattle. She sees it; it interests her. Then you place your hand in front of it, preventing her from reaching and grasping it directly. If her response to the problem is to push aside your hand, her action is fully intentional.

I often sit on the sofa at home with my legs up on the coffee table. At five months, if my daughter Beth wanted to get a toy on the other side of me, she would show anger and frustration. By eight months or so she would not even bother to climb over my legs, but would simply crawl under them and get the toy. In that instance, Beth showed evidence of a preestablished means to attaining a goal, that is, of fully intentional action.

> **Try to engage your baby in plenty of activities to enrich her thinking about "if-this-then-that" concepts; nurture her understanding of means-ends relationships.**

Here are a few simple ideas:

» Attach a strand of ribbon to a rattle and place the strand in the baby's hand. Now help her pull on the strand, causing the rattle to shake and draw closer and closer to her. In the beginning, be sure she is aware of the rattle, that is, that she sees and hears it being dragged forward. Later, you can repeat this game, but hide the rattle under a cover and then pull it. This will strengthen two different schemes: means-ends and the concept that a vanished object has some permanence in the world. A game that establishes the difference between means and ends and the relationship between them will provide practice for an ability that is developing on its own as baby interacts with her immediate environment. A small pull toy has the same effect.

» Hang a rod and frame toy across the rails the of crib with handles to pull.

» Jack-in-the-box—help baby play the game.

» Hand cars and trucks—to push around smooth surfaces.

» Large striped balls—to roll around.

» Stacking blocks—build a tower and knock it down.

» Wind-up toys—help baby wind toy and release.

These kinds of activities foster several developing abilities. For example, the child discovers cause and effect in realizing she can cause the bell to ring.

Other games along these lines include the following:

« Music boxes are wonderful at this stage. Does your baby realize that the box must be wound in order for the music to play?

« At nine months, your baby enjoys playing pat-a-cake and similar games. Speak in clear sentences. Use rhymes and rhythm games.

« Expose your baby to rhythm instruments—drums, xylophones, etc. Will he make the connection between hitting/shaking and the noise?

« Roll a ball out of reach. Encourage your baby to get the ball and bring it back to you.

» Place three blocks in a row and encourage your baby to push them around. Maybe he will realize that pushing the end block makes all the others move as well.

» Hand your baby a toy but continue to hold one end of it. Does he try to hit your hand to make you release the object? The purpose is for baby to realize that your hands as well as his can be used as a means to an end.

IMITATION

The Stage IV baby shows considerable progress in the area of imitation. Consider this example: At about eight months of age, my daughter Beth would vocalize various sounds. One day I heard her saying "a-wa-wa" over and over. I repeated it immediately, several times. She looked up at me, and once I stopped, she started to imitate me. I quickly changed the utterance to "a-wa-wa-wa." Again she stopped and noticed the change. When I stopped, she took her turn, imitating what I had done. The important features of this imitation were that it involved parts of her body she couldn't see (her tongue and mouth) and that she could reproduce someone else's new sounds.

If you bend your finger in a certain way, your baby will try to approximate the action. The closest he will come will be to wave his arm! Still, this shows that your child is now aware of the movements of his own body as well as the movements of others. Although Beth could not see her tongue and mouth movements in relation to mine, she could feel them. She made a connection between what she had seen me do and what she could not see herself do.

An infant is only capable of imitating movements that are familiar actions already in her repertoire. Furthermore, an infant's initial attempts at imitation are usually only approximate reproductions.

So baby now has improved memory for concrete events and can imitate actions and sounds that took place earlier. She can also postpone an action that she had initiated, pay attention to another event, and then resume her action pattern again. She will enjoy playing the following imitation games.

« Make faces, wait for imitation. Also: Repeat sounds that baby utters. Change the number of times you repeat the sound uttered, the length of the utterance, etc.

« Point to and name objects in picture books while telling the story.

» Encourage baby to feed you, wipe your face with a towel, etc.

» Scratch your head dramatically, exaggerating the motions. Wait for the imitation.

» Give your baby a block or paper tube. Dial the phone. Does he try to imitate your actions? Later on, does he try to imitate you, using a toy telephone? Does he try to imitate your playing the piano? Try hugging a stuffed animal. Does he stop what he is doing in order to watch you, then return to his previous activity?

» Can your baby imitate you blowing air through a straw?

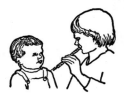

Earlier your baby could only imitate actions already in his repertoire. Now your baby can start to imitate your original actions. Be inventive and give him plenty to choose from.

- Yawn.
- Wave bye-bye.
- Clap your hands.
- Make animal noises.
- Stick out your tongue.
- Rub your eyes.
- Touch your toes.

ANTICIPATION

Another Stage IV attainment is an infant's increasing ability to anticipate events. The babysitter has come into the house, and Mommy is putting on her coat: she will be going soon! Perhaps if one cries loud enough...

Anticipations result from established routines. Certain visual cues or other stimuli alert your baby to a familiar pattern and signal a forthcoming event.

One of my students at UCLA reported the following routines with her baby. When preparing to make her bed in the morning, she would put the pillows at the foot of the bed and fluff them up. Her son, Andrew, would squeal with delight each day as he slapped the pillows. When Andy saw his mother preparing to make the bed, he eagerly awaited the pillows at the foot of the bed so he could slap and fluff! Whenever she changed Andy's diaper or dressed him on the changing table, she turned on the tape recorder located behind the changing table. If she did not turn the tape on immediately, Andy would turn his head, looking directly at the tape recorder. Andy anticipated. He was able to organize or coordinate two schemes (action patterns) together. Diaper changing was accompanied by music.

Setting up routines and playing the same games over and over again helps nurture the concept of anticipation. For example, playing tickle games such as "this little piggy" tends to stimulate the sense of anticipation.

Beth enjoyed playing the "attack" game: I would make an airplane noise and gradually "attack," with my head ending up in her lap. It was certainly fun for both of us. Yet at the same time she was firmly constructing the concept of anticipation: the moment I made the whining sound of the airplane engine, she would perk up and prepare for the game.

» Hold your baby on your lap and drop a toy on the floor, then ask the baby "Where did the toy go?" This simple game will stimulate the sense of prevision and reinforce the notion of anticipation.

» Make daily routines into exciting learning experiences. For example, in the supermarket, have your baby help you place things in the cart. Point out color, size, texture (fruits and vegetables are good for this), and the pictures on the boxes. This will help him to connect the picture on the outside with the object on the inside.

« Can your baby anticipate events? Walk toward him with a bib and put it on him. Does he squeal, elevate his shoulders, etc. in anticipation of meal time? Approach him with a favorite toy. Does he get excited as he concentrates on the object?

PHYSICAL CAUSALITY

Before Stage IV, you may have thought to yourself that your baby seemed—to use an admittedly adult way of looking at things—self-centered or even egocentric. And, to our way of thinking, at least, this was a very accurate analysis. After all, if we meet an adult who seems to believe that his actions and only his actions cause things to occur, we consider the person rather self-absorbed. That self-absorption is the frame of reference your baby has been operating under for the first three stages.

In Stage IV, for the first time, your baby becomes aware that *objects* can cause actions to occur, or that another person can initiate an event. This is not to say that the Stage IV baby is the picture of altruism; far from it. However, the egocentricity does seem to have receded noticeably. This is because the world as experienced by your baby has taken on an entirely new feel since his discovery that he is not the only one who initiates action.

I once played a game with Beth in which I lightly pinched her nose and said "honk, honk." When I removed my hand, she would quickly grab it and place it on her nose so that I would repeat the game. She had obviously established a cause-effect connection: she realized that the cause was pinching the nose, and the effect was saying "honk, honk."

» Similarly, if your son realizes that you have to wind a wind-up toy in order to make it perform, then he has realized a cause-effect relation that goes beyond his causing an event. Your winding the toy (cause) makes the toy perform (effect). For the very first time, causality has been externalized.

 In Stage IV, your child constructs the idea that objects and other people can be the source of causality, and that he does not have to be the source of all causality.

In the course of time children build these and many more concepts as they interact with things and people. Through various kinds of physical experiences and social interactions, they construct an understanding of scientific and mathematical concepts and create knowledge of the social world surrounding them, picking up language, cultural expectations, daily routines, and other rules and regulations.

Prior to the onset of language, babies are enormously busy with the task of constructing a basic understanding of the physical, mathematical, and conventional world in which they live. They do this, we must remember, by acting on things and seeing other people acting on things. Nowhere in this interaction does the parent tell a child, for instance, how to construct a concept of causality. Being told is not how babies learn; they must do.

This is why I place such emphasis on creative "thinking games"; they engage children in interactions that nurture their development. These games strengthen an infant's natural tendencies toward building ways of knowing.

Here are a few game suggestions appropriate for helping to develop the sense of physical causality.

« Roll a ball (one roughly the size of a volleyball) to knock down a doll as your baby watches.

« Strike a little drum—baby will connect your arm movements to the sound produced by them.

« Make marks on a small chalkboard.

« Let the child turn the dial on an old radio to change the station.

» Assist in playing with toy trucks
and cars.

OBJECT CONCEPT

In Stage IV, somewhere between the age of eight to ten
months, baby reaches a milestone: He finally masters the
concept of the permanence of objects. When an object
vanishes from his field of vision, he will search for it
both visually and manually. Suppose that you drop a toy
in front of your son and immediately cover it with a
handkerchief.

» Will he remove the hanky and retrieve
the toy?

» Is he aware that even though the toy
is not in his field of vision, it still exists?

» Does he know that a vanished object
has a permanence all its own—independent of his direct perception of it?

The answer to these questions is now "yes." In Stage
III, baby's object concept was developing and was evi-
denced by a limited visual search for the vanished object. It had not yet matured to the point where manual
search was possible. Now babies demonstrate their understanding that objects can exist independently of their
own direct perception of them.

« Interestingly, this ability has certain limitations. Suppose, when you and your daughter are playing with blocks, she sees you put some blocks in the side compartment of her rolling toy cart. At this stage she will lift the cart top and retrieve the blocks. But if you were first to put the blocks in the cart, then remove them, and then put them under a blanket, with baby watching you the entire time, she would be unable to retrieve the blocks from the second hiding place.

We describe this limitation by saying that in Stage IV, *sequential displacement* has not yet developed. Remember, ideas are not mastered instantaneously. It will take some time for the baby to refine her perceptions of the world. Maturing infants need practice in manually searching for objects in order for the object concept to develop to the next level of sophistication.

Again, peek-a-boo type games are an excellent way to enrich the concept of object permanence. A word of caution: be careful not to startle your baby by placing her blanket over her head.

« Start by hiding an object in a cooking pot with a cover and letting baby retrieve it.

» Put a ticking clock under her blanket
and let her search for and uncover it.

» Wrap a noise-making toy (a rattle or
a bell, for instance) in a piece of paper
or a piece of cloth, then, with baby's
help, unwrap it. Never, never use plastic
wrap, however. It could cause suffocation.

» Hide objects as baby tracks them
visually. Let her find them.

» Use "nesting" toys—for instance,
cups that fit into one another. Or use
a series of concentric cylinders that col-
lapse into one another and pull out to
form a cone.

« Supervise while baby places small objects in a jar and removes them. Vary the game by using a pot, a bag, or a shoe box.

« Use the cardboard cylinder from a roll of paper towels and slip a colorful handkerchief through one end and out the other. Help baby see and do that too.

« Use different barriers in covering objects. Try boxes, books, paper, blankets, clothes, pans, pillows, cups, stuffed animals, entire body, legs, etc. Also try placing the barrier so that if your baby knocks too hard, the toy will fall out of reach. This will help him learn to control his arm movements.

« In peek-a-boo games, place a doll under a blanket so that its shape is visible. Later try placing the doll under a box so it is completely hidden. Will your baby search for it?

» Put an object in a paper bag, then a cloth bag, then a shoe box, then a round box. Let your baby watch you find the object. Repeat the procedure and see if he makes any gestures to find the object himself. Try dropping the toy into a sock.

» Play hide-and-seek by placing a rattle under a box and shaking the rattle gently. Does this help your baby to search for the object?

» Play hide-and-seek with a matchbox that slides in and out. This a more complicated variation on the theme.

» Clothes will provide many interesting opportunities for peek-a-boo activities as they are taken off and put on the child. By the way, it may be frustrating from your point of view, but the child who takes off his diapers and pants is demonstrating a new ability to remove barriers.

Baby's intelligent actions cannot be performed in a vacuum; they must be performed on what I have referred to as "objects of knowledge." Space and time are also objects of knowledge. Here are some games you can try at this stage to enhance baby's understanding of how objects behave in space and in time. (If you are thinking to yourself that this sounds like the beginnings of physics, you're right!)

« Fill up and empty boxes.

« Cut a hole in the top of a large coffee can and work with your baby in dropping cereal or large (non-swallowable) buttons inside.

« Give your baby sponges in the bathtub to play with.

COORDINATING AND CONSOLIDATING

The Stage IV baby is very busy coordinating the secondary circular reactions acquired in previous stages. This is a conservative time in terms of mental development, because baby is less interested in learning new schemes than in discovering applications to new situations using known schemes. These coordinated secondary reactions result in more elaborate versions of the actions of the previous stage. They are more intentional.

This is an opportunity to help baby consolidate past experiences. If we remain aware of the progression of an infant's abilities, we can do a great deal to influence its direction and help coordinate and consolidate baby's advancing ways of knowing.

SUMMARY OF INTELLECTUAL ATTAINMENTS
(STAGE IV: Eight through twelve months)

Intellectual Activity

END OF EIGHTH MONTH

Actions become fully intentional.

Conceives goal first, then seeks means of attaining it.

Explores objects appreciating their own existence.

Manually searches for hidden objects when watching them being hidden. Has not yet mastered "sequential displacements."

Isolates means from ends.

Solves simple means-ends problems.

Has rudimentary concept of number: one item vs. more than one—a qualitative idea only.

Begins to anticipate events. Can tell when you are leaving because you are putting your coat on; can tell it is bath time when hears water in tub; and so on.

Has improved memory for concrete events; imitates actions and sounds that took place earlier.

Deferred circular reaction (stops doing something to attend to something else then goes back to activity).

Begins to see self as means to an end. Kicks in an effort to move or get object. Pulls to obtain certain result, etc.

END OF NINTH MONTH

Maturing object concept—knows object will reappear.

Establishing self as causal agent.

END OF TENTH MONTH

Manually searches for vanished object as it disappears before him.

Imitates regularly observed acts.

Perceives self as separate from other objects.

Anticipates.

END OF ELEVENTH MONTH / BEGINNING OF TWELFTH MONTH

Experiments with object-space relations.

Imitates more subtle movements.

Nests things into one another.

Images some events.

Age approximations are intended as guidelines only. Please regard them as rough estimates.

CHAPTER NINE

◆

Stage V
(12 to 18 Months)
Discovering New Means

◆

Happy BIRTHDAY!

Congratulations to you and your child. Throughout this year your baby has steadily progressed from a state of near-total helplessness to one of dawning mental awareness of his surrounding physical and social world. Put more simply, he is now a toddler.

He is beginning to walk, talk, and even solve problems on a sensorimotor level. Having reached these milestones, we have only two infant stages left to discuss, Stages V and VI—probably the most extraordinary periods of all. By the conclusion of Stage V, your baby will display his first authentic, purposeful, individually creative experimentation. His entry to Stage VI will mark the beginning of what we can legitimately call independent thought.

TERTIARY CIRCULAR REACTIONS

Watch your baby drop a spoon or some other object and pick it up again. Notice how this action is repeated over and over again; each time baby concentrates on the way he releases the spoon and where it lands.

He is engaging in a process of trying to understand; what I refer to as the "know-how of experimentation." He systematically varies previously learned and well-patterned behavior to discover what the new results might be. Already familiar with the outcome of a given sequence of behavior, small procedural changes are made in an effort to see the effect of these variations.

Piaget labeled the fifth stage of infant mental development the stage of *tertiary circular reactions*—that stage in which an intense interest in novelty for its own sake makes the child repeat his actions on certain objects. Look closely at your child's actions, and you will agree that it is because of his interest in novelty that he varies his acts each time with slight modification. He has become a dauntless researcher, resorting to unending trial and error to test final results.

Tertiary circular reactions are intentional, repetitive, experimental action patterns. The child causes something to happen accidentally but repeats the action by deliberately and systematically varying it to monitor, not simply "what will happen" but expected *changes* in outcome.

Gone are the days of repeating actions simply to observe an unexpected result. The vital issue on the child's mind now is how he has affected the outside world.

While secondary circular reactions were meant to consolidate the processes of experimentation, tertiary circular reactions extend them in an effort to find limits. In how many different situations does a certain sequence of actions accomplish something? How can you adapt a sequence of actions to fit other situations?

These are profound questions for your child, and he toils ceaselessly now to find answers to them. Here's what you can do to enrich this experimental bent in your baby.

» At this age, your baby likes to throw things. Play a game where you set an object on the corner of his playpen so that he can knock it off. Then you retrieve it, and repeat the game, placing the object elsewhere on the next turn. Try to vary the weights of the different objects.

» Place a ball in the end of an old nylon stocking and swing it around in front of your baby. This is the inertia concept. Does your baby try to swing it too?

» Set up a variety of inclines and provide your baby with some rolling objects (balls and cars).

» Provide a variety of building materials: books, cardboard paper tubes, blocks, foam shapes, etc.

« Encourage your baby to discover physical resistance by taking him outside and rolling a ball in the grass, where it doesn't roll as well. Also, try dropping different types of balls on different surfaces like shag rugs, plastic placemats, smooth sheets, gravel, etc.

« Cut out pictures of everyday objects such as apples, balls, and cups. Then place the actual objects by the pictures. Can you help him to match real objects with their pictures?

« Place a toy on a towel so that your baby must tug on the towel to get the object.

« Introduce a screw top jar for filling/emptying, opening/closing.

» Water play: In a sandbox or at the kitchen sink, experiment with pouring water and sand/mud.

» Can your baby slide beads on a straw?

» Children at this stage enjoy playing with quantities of the same item. Try to accommodate this by giving your baby several pillows or balls, lots of large buttons, spools, jar lids, etc.

PROBLEM SOLVING BY DISCOVERY

Baby displays intelligence by discovering entirely new sequences of actions in order to solve problems.

Place a toy on a blanket in front of your son with the toy about three feet away, then restrain him so he can't get the toy. What will he do? First he'll try to get it directly by reaching for it. Having failed, he may then pull the blanket toward himself and grab the toy! If you place another toy on the blanket, he'll go through the same motions, trying to reach for the object first, then resorting to his more elaborate scheme of pulling the blanket to get the toy.

Stage V behavior seems systematic: an entirely intellectualized form of action. It is intentional, purposeful, original, and adaptive.

Discovering new sequences of actions in an effort to deal with new situations is what this stage is all about. This is the beginning of creative and internally intelligent behavior.

Obviously, children are not always able to solve problems with foresight. What happens when they encounter the more difficult problems? Now they can resort to trial-and-error, a kind of learning that had not been available to them up to now.

Experimentation is the order of the day. When baby is faced with a problem that cannot be solved by inventing a new sequence of behavior through foresight and pre-planning, he experiments in a hit-or-miss format until he stumbles upon a solution. This is not to suggest that the activity is mindless. It involves a strategy of experimenting with alternative solutions that maximizes the chances of success through physical groping. In this sense our one-year-old begins to show the characteristics of a true problem solver!

An example may help us to understand this process. Writing about his daughter Jacqueline when she was about fifteen months of age, Piaget observed what happened when she threw a stuffed dog outside the bars of her playpen. While attempting to reach for the stuffed animal she inadvertently pushed the playpen in the right direction. Then she inadvertently moved it in the wrong direction, away from the dog. She immediately set the playpen back on course and got the dog. Jacqueline used her fortuitous discoveries to invent a new way of reaching a goal. Trial and error were shaped into a new yet systematic effort.

You can encourage your baby at this stage by helping her discover the workings of

- Hammer boards
- Merry-go-rounds
- "Corn popper" push toys
- Pop-up men
- Pinwheels

INTENTION AND MEANS-ENDS RELATIONS

In the toy-on-the-blanket example, the baby demonstrated an intentional plan to use a specific means in order to attain his goal.

 The Stage V baby carries out some kind of action and interprets the results according to what he already knows. Never passive, he continually monitors the results of his actions and adapts subsequent actions accordingly.

Your baby will show countless examples of such action at this stage; you probably encounter a number of them every day without thinking. Make a conscious effort to notice the processes at work.

« You may want, for instance, to repeat the event we examined earlier in the book of trying to hand a child a toy horizontally so that it is blocked by the vertical slats of his crib. Eventually, after a chance rotation of the object, your baby will become quite adept at bringing the toy in.

He faces a major limitation, however: he is able to experiment successfully *only* after chance success. In other words, only after he stumbles upon a solution does he become aware of that solution. This stumbling, however, is the final step toward the ability to think out the solution to a sensorimotor problem beforehand and solve the problem—a characteristic of the next and final stage of sensorimotor development.

Bear in mind the emergent nature of Stage V skills: your child's way of problem solving is not an instant reaction, as yours is, but a steadily more proficient series of adaptations. With what kinds of games, toys, and other play can you engage your child to nurture this aspect of his intellect?

IMITATION

At this stage your toddler can imitate better than ever before. If you deliberately and slowly touch your forehead as she watches, she will try to touch her own forehead the same way. If you repeat this activity again the next day, you will see her imitate you very efficiently.

In Stage IV your baby had started to imitate your behavior. So long as the behavior was not too different from her own spontaneous behavior, she was able to approximate yours, but rarely was she able to do it on the first try. She had to go through a number of tries before coming close to your action. Now, however, she is able to imitate behavior that is entirely new to her. And she is far more systematic and more proficient. She doesn't stumble onto the act that she is trying to imitate. Notice that once she learns to imitate an act or a rhyme or both together, she will want to repeat it over and over again.

To imitate, your baby has to mentally represent a model's actions. She must adapt to the situation by changing herself in the face of the present conditions, something far more difficult than simply adding to what she already can do.

> In imitating a new action, your child can't merely add to what she already can do—she must change the structure of what she knows.

Here are some ideas to consider when encouraging your child to imitate:

» *Patty-cake (pat-a-cake)*. Go through the rhyming song with motions and see your child imitate what you say and what you do.

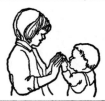

« *"Here we go round the mulberry bush!"* This song promotes coordination of the spoken word with hand and body gestures. With your child seated in front of you, sing, "This is the way we touch our nose, touch our nose, touch our nose..." Name different parts of your face as you continue. You can create countless variations on this theme. "This is the way we blink our eyes, blink our eyes, blink our eyes..." etc. It forces baby to consciously and deliberately imitate various body movements.

« Can your baby imitate you wrapping/unwrapping objects or opening/closing zippers?

« Encourage rhythm instrument imitations. You chime the triangle three times; how does your baby respond? Sing to him and vary the rhythm of the song; how does he respond?

« Does your baby try to imitate chores such as dusting, vacuuming, dish washing, setting the table?

STAGE V KNOWING: CAUSALITY, TIME, AND SPACE

Suppose you give your baby a plastic jar with an interesting toy inside it. She tries unsuccessfully to open it. Then she holds out the jar and urges you to open it, but you pay no attention to her. Chances are she will take your hand and place the jar in it so that you will open the jar for her.

In this stage your child has mastered the idea that other people as well as other objects can cause results. She even solicits the help of others in solving problems. She has differentiated the means to an end to such an extent that she now realizes she can use someone else as her means to attain a goal. Now you can also expect your toddler to involve you in her games—to intervene whenever she cannot reach an object, for instance. She will gesture and call out to you to retrieve an object or place it somewhere.

In Stage V objects as well as people are seen as potential instruments to an end. How can you get involved? Start by rmembering that for the toddler between the ages of twelve and eighteen months, toys take on immense importance. Your toddler is ready and looking for occasions to play. Stage-appropriate toys are enormously valuable now. A few suggestions:

» *Shape sorters.* Challenge a child to place certain geometric shaped objects into holes of the same shapes. This will strengthen the understanding of one's self as someone who can cause things to happen. Opening and closing the shape sorter to retrieve the objects affords trial and error learning and reinforces the notion of object, space, time, and causality.

« *Peg people or peg animals.* Made from wood or plastic, these can be transported in a small pull truck with wheels.

« *Popper beads.* Large, colorful plastic beads that fit into each other and pop out when separated.

« *Simple puzzles.* Puzzles with a few large pieces help the child learn about spatial relations. Try to get the kind with little knobs on the pieces for the child to lift and hold.

« *A set of wooden blocks.*

« *A set of plastic measuring cups for water.*

» *A sand box.*

» *Graduated colorful plastic rings that fit onto a post.*

» *A pounding wood bench with mallet.*

» *A scooter.* The ones children push with both feet on the floor are best.

« *A doll carriage.*

This list is simply to call your attention to the kinds of things a child between twelve and eighteen months enjoys the most, as well as those that provide opportunities to advance intellectual skills during playtime. Many other toys can be "manufactured" at home. For instance:

« Attach a piece of rope to a shoe box as a pull truck.

« Allow your child to play with rice and some safe pots and pans.

« Provide a large cardboard box to crawl in and out of.

» Cut a circle the size of a ping-pong ball in the plastic top of a coffee can. Provide three ping-pong balls and three blocks to be used as sorters.

» Use plastic cups and other plastic containers at bath time to encourage water pouring.

» Stacking toys is an excellent activity. Stack some blocks. Will the child reach for a colored one in the middle?

» Spatial relations: Color one side of a cardboard tube. Will your baby turn it in order to see the colored side?

» Supply your child with large plastic nuts and bolts to encourage screwing these on and off. These will also be good if he likes to try imitating household activities that use these tools.

« Drop clothespins into transparent bottles; drop cars into large envelopes.

« For nesting toys, try using paper cups or shoe boxes.

STAGE V: THE OBJECT CONCEPT

In Stage IV, if you hid an object in one place then moved it to a second, then a third spot, your baby looked for the object where it was last discovered. In Stage V, however, babies can finally follow a hidden object through a series of displacements.

This is a very important advancement. To identify the object with the place where it was last discovered means that the child has formed a simple connection between the object and its place. But to understand that the last place it was *discovered* doesn't necessarily matter—because it may have moved to another place—implies a new and enlarged understanding of the ways objects exist in the world.

This advance in representational thought is in many ways exactly what your child has been working toward for all these months. It signifies a wholly different type of intelligence.

Still, there is much growing to be done. Following a sequence of displacements is impressive, but it is only the threshold of a completely mature form of object permanence. As yet, these displacements must be visible in order for the child to follow them. If we place a toy inside a box, for example, then place the box behind a screen and remove the toy from the box, the child will not think to look behind the screen when handed the empty container. It will be another few months before he can do that. Stage VI (between the ages of eighteen months and two years) is the period in which baby fully masters the object concept—thinking about things even when they are not there or even when they are moved from place to place. He will have outgrown sensorimotor intelligence and entered a form of knowing in which it is possible to form mental images of things. This will enable him to have an image *stand for* the real thing.

In Stages III and IV peek-a-boo games were totally appropriate play because the child was in the process of constructing the concept of the permanence of objects. Your child found it remarkable that an object could disappear one moment only to return the next. His expectation was that a disappearing object had completely vanished. Why and how did it reappear? That puzzle created an intense interest in peek-a-boo games.

At a certain point, a child's interest in these types of games begins to wane. Now he knows that the hidden object is to be found somewhere. The reappearance of the object is no longer mysterious. In Stage V, however, we move into games of hide and seek. The child now knows that the object must be somewhere. The challenge is to find it. Hide and seek is not much fun before this stage because the expectation of finding the hidden object is not yet a certainty. Games you can play to enhance this new ability include:

- *Hide and seek.* Hide a toy then join your baby in look-ing for it.
- *Crumpling paper.* The process of crumpling is fasci-nating for your baby to watch ; if you then place the ball of paper in a bucket (perhaps also containing a small toy), will the baby be interested in finding it?
- Continue playing with the jack-in-the-box.
- "Read" books together. Laminated cardboard pages of rhymes, songs, and simple stories are the best.
- Hide behind a door, leaving your head partially ex-posed. Encourage baby to find you, and delight in her success.
- Play reverse hide and seek. Let baby "hide" and you "try" to find him. Pretend you can't find him ini-tially, then do. Try using a large cardboard box as a hiding place for your baby while you go hunting for him.

LANGUAGE

By the first birthday, it is not unusual for a baby to have a vocabulary of three or four words. She acts in response to speech, comes when called, understands commands, babbles expressively, and looks in specific places when asked where some object or person is. By the time she is two years old, the number of words she will have mas-tered will be somewhere between 200 and 1,000.

From this point forward, vocabulary acquisition becomes very rapid indeed!

Meaningful verbal interactions during this period, al-though they need not be not censored in any way, should have the following emphasis.

- Encourage baby to use social words: bye-bye, love you, etc.
- Use action words to describe the child's actions.
- Point to and name objects in the baby's immediate environment.
- React with enthusiasm to baby's efforts to talk; smile and repeat baby's words.

FROM NEWBORN TO TODDLER

Your child has come a long way. The toddler between the age of one year and eighteen months can walk, talk a little, and problem-solve through trial and error—quite efficiently too. He experiments. He intentionally and systematically varies an action to discover how the differences change the outcomes. He understands that not only he but other people and objects can cause things to happen. He has constructed some idea of time, space, and how objects fit in and out of other things. He knows that if a toy has been moved from one hiding place to another—and another—he should look for it in the place where he last saw it. He can imitate new and novel acts.

Your toddler is on his way to moving beyond sensorimotor intelligence, which, though it has served him well, is a knowledge system restricted to what can be touched, seen, heard, smelled, and tasted. He is beginning to develop the capacity to represent objects and events mentally—to have a symbolic system. He is able to know things by imaging them, to use his intelligence thoughtfully, as only human beings can.

SUMMARY OF INTELLECTUAL ACTIVITIES
(STAGE V: Twelve to eighteen months)

Note: abilites develop with great variety among Stage V children; month divisions for the achievements at this stage are less useful than in the previous ones.

Ability

Discovers new sequences of actions in order to solve problems.

Capable of trial and error learning.

Systematically and intentionally varies actions to discover how variations change outcome.

Sees objects and people as instruments to goal.

Enjoys discovering spatial relations.

Sense of physical causality improves.

Object concept improves.

Imitation improves.

Early language skills develop.

◆

CHAPTER   TEN

Stage VI
(18 to 24 Months)
Inventing Through Mental
Combinations

◆

THE KEYSTONE OF INDEPENDENT, symbolic human thought can be found in two awe-inspiring words: *what if ... ?* The words themselves are not accountable for the remarkable progress your child makes during Stage VI, but the incredibly powerful concept they represent most certainly is.

What if your child could use mental symbols to represent things that are absent from his view? What if he could mentally represent the external world through memory, imagery, symbols and abbreviated actions? And what if he could symbolically combine these features of mental growth to reach a desired goal?

You would be witnessing the birth of symbolic thought. This is the level of attainment your toddler has reached and is beginning to use on his own. There is a world of possibilities available to him now, including (but by no means limited to), deferred imitation, imagination, and creative "let's pretend" play.

SYMBOLIC THOUGHT

This new "what if" development heralds the start of a cognitive revolution that frees your child from the constraints of the here and now. This liberation will have dramatic and far-reaching consequences, and will, by the end of Stage VI, ignite nothing less than an explosion of mental power.

> **We can now truly say that the child has the ability to think, not just the ability to produce intelligent actions.**

How do we know that your baby is capable of this mental representation? The Stage VI child can perform two important acts indicating attainment of the symbolic system:

1. He can solve problems without engaging in trial and error, i.e., without direct, physical groping.
2. He can postpone imitating an observed behavior until a later time.

PROBLEM SOLVING THROUGH INVENTION

If baby Christy can solve simple problems without the physical groping and trial and error associated with Stage V, then she *must* be figuring things out in her head before applying her conclusions. Suppose she sees, for the first time, an interesting-looking marionette resting on top of the bookshelf in her room. A thin, loose string hangs from the figure and dangles just out of reach.

Christy walks to the bookcase, turns over a nearby milk-crate normally used to store toys, stands on it, grasps the string, and pulls the marionette to the floor.

There is no experimenting at all here; Christy did not go through a series of failed attempts to get the marionette. She saw the problem, constructed a solution, and implemented it. The "what if" instinct operated flawlessly.

Physical groping has been replaced by mental groping. Not surprisingly, the Stage VI child reaches solutions much faster than the Stage V child.

At this stage of your child's development, your goal should be to provide your toddler with the fullest and richest play opportunities possible. Wherever you can, let your child initiate the activities. Let them be spontaneous, self-chosen, and, above all, fun. Any other course is to attempt to impose something on the child's intellect, and this will bore and frustrate him.

Here are a few suggestions:

» Push and pull toys provide occasions for problem solving. What happens when an obstacle blocks the toy's path, or an object keeps falling off its resting place as it moves?

» Simple puzzles engage the child's ability to reason out what fits where.

« Nesting toys encourage the child to figure out what goes into what, or what must be stacked on what.

« Shape sorters activate problem-solving techniques involving geometric forms.

DELAYED IMITATION

« One day, three-year-old Janet and her mother come to visit you and your child. Noticing how much attention your child receives, the older Janet decides to pound a certain toy on the high-chair tray. A few days later, your child, alone with you, decides to pound away on her own high chair with the toy in her hand! Janet is not present; somehow your child stored the event and now decides to retrieve it.

Deferred imitation is convincing evidence of the baby's ability to symbolize things: to store an act, a phrase, or a game in memory and, at an appropriate later time, to retrieve it and act it out.

Here are a few enjoyable and enriching imitation activities that are helpful in Stage VI.

» Toy telephones—and later on, real ones—encourage verbal exchange and imitation of adults or siblings.

» Wearing adult clothes to "assume" different social roles encourages children to accommodate themselves to various forms of social behavior.

» Pretend games nurture imitatative acts and encourage children to assume someone else's feelings and actions. And pretending that one is asleep, sneezing, coughing, or yawning is more than mere fun—it means accommodating oneself to a different situation. Playing with dolls and puppets represent the same type of action.

» Dancing provides musical fun and increases consciousness of one's own body.

« Imitate object/animal sounds, such as bird, cats, trucks, trains, etc.

« Give your baby a paintbrush and a bucket of water and encourage him to "help" you complete a painting job.

« Encourage your child to imitate/ help out in the garden.

STAGE VI KNOWLEDGE: TIME, SPACE, CAUSALITY, AND THE OBJECT CONCEPT

» Jacqueline throws a ball under a sofa. Without hesitation, she sets out to look for it behind the sofa. This incident illustrates Jacqueline's maturing conceptual development. It demonstrates her ability to mentally represent things and their displacements in space. Not only does she realize that the object has a permanence of its own, but she can imagine the *invisible* displacements taking place as the ball travels under the sofa and comes to rest behind it.

In addition to showing a mature object concept, this example typifies the Stage VI child's ability to combine concepts of time, space, causality, and object permanence to yield an expectation of where the ball *should* be.

Your toddler demonstrates his understanding of space and spatial relations in many different ways every day. He opens a gate in order to get past a fence; when you and he return from the grocery store, he points in recognition to *his* house as you approach it on the road.

» Nicole clearly understands cause-effect relations when she looks for an explanation as to why a wind-up toy continues its action.

« With your hands hidden from your child's sight behind a pillow, manipulate a puppet back and forth. Your child's first reaction is to look at you in awe. Have you anything at all to do with the event?

Of course, we can't expect a mature understanding of time, space, causality, or object concept at two years of age; this understanding develops continually. The science of physics (which we discussed briefly in an earlier chapter) formalizes these concepts and extends them to their theoretical limits. Your Stage VI youngster is not yet an accomplished physicist, but he is a budding one!

Although his ideas about the physical world may seem strange to you at times, they are utterly sensible in light of his experience. He may blink to turn the lights on, bang his foot against the floor to make the window open wider, and move his own hand to make mommy move hers.

Most of what you did with your child in Stage V will be equally interesting and enjoyable in Stage VI. You may also want to introduce some new toys and games that are both appropriate and exciting in this, the final stage of the sensorimotor period. Here are a few examples.

« Finger paints

» More baby books. Picture books are wonderful for this age; they help teach language skills. When using animal picture books, make the sounds that the animals make. Stress colors, shapes, and sounds, when reading through the books with your child.

» Play dough.

» Sand and water play.

» Body parts. Point out your child's ears, eyes, nose, etc., talking about the function of each part. Cover your baby's eyes, then mouth, etc. Then cover your own. Keep taking turns. This helps your toddler begin to realize that each body part has a certain function.

« Allow your baby to fill plastic milk bottles with sand, water, pebbles, or Cheerios, and then empty them.

« Use squeeze bottles in the bathtub to encourage experimentation.

« Purchase or make a "do-it-myself board" with hinges, knobs, locks, etc.

« To encourage detailed finger movements, let your infant help you in the kitchen by giving him a banana to peel.

Also—try a puzzle or two:

» When playing with blocks, pick one up and show it to your baby. Ask your baby to hand you a block 'just like' the one you are holding. Use color, size, and texture, but remember to vary only one feature at a time.

» Sit on the floor with your baby with both of your legs apart and your feet touching. Roll a ball between you.

» Use simple, store-bought peg puzzles. Your child is ready for puzzles with five to seven pieces.

» Provide more complex block sets with several varying shapes and sizes. Allow him to play freely with these.

» Push/pull and carry games are wonderful for this stage.

« At the age of two, most children are ready for make-believe games. Encourage them!

« Provide your child with paper and crayons for scribbling.

« Roughhouse activities are suitable at this stage.

« Help your child make a collage out of everyday materials such as paper, fabric scraps, yarn, and popcorn.

« Give your baby a cloth toy with lots of different closings: hooks, buttons, zippers, flaps, and pockets.

» At this age your baby will like toys with hidden parts that disappear when knobs are turned, etc.

» Your baby likes to play with knobs, keys, and buttons, so try to find little cash registers, telephones, and similar toys.

» Use time concepts: "Today we will ... Tomorrow... Yesterday... Now ..."

» Practice stringing beads of different shapes (spheres, cubes, etc.)

» Play magnet games on the refrigerator.

« Let your child experiment with a magnifying glass.

« Supply your child with more complicated nesting toys.

« Hold up a large piece of newspaper and encourage your baby to punch a hole through the paper. Try crumpling the paper and playing with the crumpled balls.

« Help your baby to throw a ball through a hula hoop. Also give your baby lots of balls (of varying sizes and textures) to practice hitting, throwing, and rolling.

« Allow your child to climb in and out of spaces.

» Drop colored clothespins into an open coffee can. Then attach the clothespins to the outside of the can.

All of these suggestions (and any more you might think of) promote the ability to interact with—and further the development of—the construction of concepts of time, space, causality, and object.

PUTTING IT ALL TOGETHER

We have arrived at the final stage of sensorimotor intelligence, a stage that designates the end of the reliance on the here and now. The process of cognitive development has brought him to a point where objects can be represented by signs or symbols. What an accomplishment!

 The concrete, empirical experience is no longer your child's primary basis of knowing.

This new development is the start of the ability to think, not just the ability to produce intelligent actions. As we have seen, your toddler can now solve problems without actually engaging in trial and error, that is, without direct, physical groping, and he can postpone imitating an observed behavior until a later time.

In Stage VI, your child is already well furnished with a multitude of schemes; all he needs is to evoke these schemes mentally. The implications of this are far-reaching. The act of deferred imitation, for instance, serves as convincing evidence of the baby's ability to symbolize things. To store an act, a phrase, a game in memory and, later, when desired, to retrieve it and act it out, is a byproduct of this newly evolved ability to symbolize things.

The concepts of object, space, time, and causality are integrated at a level that enables the child to construct her own reality of the world around her. Not only does she realize that the object has a permanence of its own, she can also imagine the invisible displacements that are occurring.

She is no longer passive, dependent, and reactive; she is a thinking person who knows she exists as one of the many entrancing elements of "the world." There are vast horizons of growth awaiting her, but she will approach them now equipped with her own unique ideas, reflections, and goals.

SUMMARY OF INTELLECTUAL ATTAINMENTS
(Stage VI: Eighteen to twenty-four months)

Note: abilites develop with great variety among Stage VI children; month divisions for the achievements at this stage are less useful than in the previous ones.

Intellectual Activities

Invents solutions before acting to solve problem.

Deferred imitation.

Follows displacements of objects as moved from place to place.

Seeks physical explanations for events.

APPENDICES

APPENDIX A

Risk Factors: An Overview

A NUMBER OF FACTORS AFFECT the development of infants, and, thereby, their later lives. In the pages following we will touch on a number of these factors.

Risk factors are many and varied. Some psychologists have simply listed such factors as drugs, diseases, and environmental influences. Others have sorted them into two categories: biological and environmental. Still others have included interactional effects stemming from a combination of biological and environmental factors.

This section is an overview of some of the more relevant issues of this rather complicated academic question. The two tables on the following pages are from Linda Smolak's fine work *Infancy* (Prentice-Hall, 1986).

PRENATAL FACTORS:
DRUGS, DISEASES, AND CERTAIN
ENVIRONMENTAL INFLUENCES

What are the risk factors with regard to drugs, diseases, and environmental influences your baby can face while still developing in the womb?

SOME POTENTIAL INFLUENCES ON PRENATAL DEVELOPMENT

Drugs

Heroin and Methadone
Potential effects: Retarded growth; withdrawal symptoms such as tremors, irritability, hyperactivity, shrill cry; SIDS (crib death)

Aspirin (large doses, last trimester)
Potential effects: Blood clotting problems for both mother and newborn

DES (a synthetic hormone frequently used between 1945 and 1970 to prevent miscarriage)
Potential effects: Abnormalities in reproductive system, including pregnancy complications and cervical cancer

Caffeine
Potential effects: Unclear; probably minimal unless combined with cigarette smoking or in very high doses

Streptomycin
Potential effects: Hearing loss

Tetracycline
Potential effects: Dental malformations

Diseases

Rubella
Potential effects: Congenital cataracts, deafness, heart disease, microcephaly, stunted growth

Syphilis
   Potential effects: Spontaneous abortion common; deafness, blindness, various malformations, mental retardation; syphilis

Herpes II
   Potential effects: Life-threatening if it infects the central nervous system during the first four weeks postnatally; transmitted during or after birth only

Diabetes
   Potential effects: Abnormally large babies, frequently resulting in delivery complications; higher rate of fetal and neonatal mortality

Environment

Stress
   Potential effects: Unclear, but perhaps Downs syndrome, pyloric stenosis, various behavior problems

Radiation (large doses)
   Potential effects: Fetal death, microcephaly, mental retardation, various malformations, possibly delayed cancers and leukemia

Mercury (ingested by eating contaminated meat or fish)
   Potential effects: Central nervous system damage manifested postnatally by tremors, convulsions, irritability, and abnormal EEG

Hot saunas (especially at 3-4 weeks of pregnancy)
   Potential effects: Anencephaly (no cortex)

Hexachlorophene (frequent exposure)
   Potential effects: Various severe malformations

As these data show, drugs, diseases and some environmental influences may have serious effects on the physical and/or intellectual development of fetuses.

PERINATAL AND POST-NATAL BIOLOGICAL FACTORS

The table on the following page offers a sketch of the relevant biological risk factors and associated outcomes for babies during and after birth.

PERINATAL AND POSTNATAL BIOLOGICAL RISK FACTORS AND THEIR ASSOCIATED OUTCOMES

Anoxia or asphyxia (oxygen deprivation at birth)
Potential effects: Most show no long-term effects but can result in brain injury, cerebral palsy, or, possibly, minimal brain dysfunction (for example, hyperactivity)

Malnutrition
Potential effects: Depends on length, duration, and severity of malnutrition; can result in apathy, overall developmental retardation, and brain dysfunction

Accidents
Potential effects: As many as 50,000 children per year may have accidents severe enough to result in neurological damage or dysfunction (for example, hyperactivity, learning problems)

Meningitis
Potential effects: Effects vary but can include brain damage, mental retardation, and hearing loss

Reyes syndrome
Effects vary but can result in mental retardation and neurological dysfunction

Lead poisoning
Depending on level of lead in bloodstream, can result in seizures, mental retardation, and behavioral disorders.

◆

Nutrition, Alcohol, and Cigarettes: Their Impact on Fetal and Infant Development

◆

ALL THE FACTORS EXAMINED on the immediately preceding pages are certainly critical. Unfortunately, for many of them parents are not in much of a position to alter the effect; we as parents do not decide to get into an automobile accident or deprive a baby of oxygen during birth. The issue of nutrition, however, *is* one that we can do something about in a preventive manner. Here are a few further thoughts about nutrition, alcohol consumption, and cigarette smoking.

NUTRITION

In his comprehensive book *The Brain: The Last Frontier,*
Dr. Richard M. Restak writes:

> The brains of children who have died of malnutri-
> tion during the first two years of life have fewer
> brain cells compared to normal children. They also
> have an overall decrease in whole brain size. In ad-
> dition, it seems not to make much difference ex-
> actly when malnutrition occurs, as long as it's
> sometime in the first two years. (Page 129.)

Dr. Restak, citing the work of Dr. Ernesto Pollitt of
the Massachusetts Institute of Technology with North
American Indian children, points out that Pollitt
"demonstrated a 50 percent decrease in behavioral
performance in severely malnutritioned children.
Memory, abstract reasoning, thinking, and verbal ability were most affected." (Page 128.)

These findings have been supported by Dr. Merrill S.
Read of the National Institute of Child Health and
Human Development. Dr. Read's conclusions are based
on observations of a group of Korean children who had
been adopted in the United States and who had been
severely malnutritioned early in life. His findings were
that "...malnutritioned children, even though they are
not retarded in later life, are never able to achieve their
full intellectual potential." (Restak, page 130.)

How widespread is malnutrition among infants?
World Health Organization estimates are that as many as
three hundred million are undernourished. As one
might expect, most of these are in developing countries.
And yet the question of nutrition is not merely an academic one for those of us in more economically advanced societies.

True, it is doubtful that many European or American
children are suffering from malnutrition as it is clinically

defined. But if nutrition in the first two years of life is so critical, it certainly behooves us to consider closely the nutritional needs of the baby *before it is born*. This, sadly, is often overlooked. Pregnant mothers should establish a sound dietary regimen in concert with a qualified pediatrician or other medical professional. Failing to do so may adversely affect the baby's developments.

CIGARETTE SMOKING AND ALCOHOL

While the effects of a mother's smoking on the intellectual development of the fetus are still very much in debate, we can make a clear connection between the mother's smoking habit and an infant's decreased birth weight.

Newborns of smoking women are an average of 200 grams (just under a half pound) lighter than newborns of nonsmokers. This trend has held steady since it was first reported in 1957. Moreover, the link holds true regardless of other variables, such as race, sex of the child, socioeconomic status, gestational age, and so on. In addition, it appears that cigarette smoking among those who are already at risk increases the probability of fetal or infant death.

As for alcohol, the Food and Drug Administration has been warning pregnant women against the use of alcohol for some time. This is because alcohol consumption has been linked with a rare but serious disease known as Fetal Alcohol Syndrome (FAS), which afflicts about 25 of every 1,000 live births. The symptoms include mental retardation, facial abnormalities, abnormal sleep patterns, etc.

Smoking, drinking alcoholic beverages, and doing drugs all are hazardous to the unborn. It is also worth noting that what a mother introduces to her system is not the only danger: high stress levels and prolonged bouts of emotional depression have also been shown to be harmful to unborn children. All of these tendencies can have very serious implications for children after birth. Some of the habits are deadly—not only to the baby but to the mother as well.

These conditions are products of one's lifestyle and can be controlled; there is simply no place in our society for poor prenatal care. It is absolutely crucial that pregnant mothers do what they can to minimize such hazardous conditions in their lives. A healthy mother gives her unborn child his best chance for healthy development, not just for today but for as long as he continues to grow.

It bears repeating. *Consult your doctor;* establish a good prenatal care regimen and follow it.

◆

Miscellaneous Environmental Risk Factors: Single Parenting/ Divorce and Daycare

◆

IN ADDITION TO BIOLOGICAL RISK FACTORS and dangers such as malnutrition and low birth weight due to the mother's smoking, there is a category of what we might call "lifestyle" environmental risk factors.

Perhaps of greatest interest in this area to today's parents are the issues of

- Single parenting

- Divorce

- Daycare

We will examine these matters in this section of the book.

The table on the following page, from Linda Smolak's *Infancy* (Prentice-Hall, 1986), will serve to provide a good overview of risk factors in the "lifestyle" category.

ENVIRONMENTAL RISK FACTORS AND THEIR ASSOCIATED OUTCOMES

War

If parents remain available and supportive, long-term effects are usually minimal. However, if child is separated from family, a variety of behavioral disorders may result.

Divorce

The outcomes for very young children do not appear to be as severe as for children over five years of age. Most children of all ages will show short-term (one-to-two-year) behavioral problems. The severity and duration of problems vary greatly depending on adjustment of parents, custody arrangements, and disruption of other aspects of family life (for example, moving or mother going to work).

Working mother

No clearly negative long-term effects of daycare have been documented. There is, however, an increased rate of illness in daycare children. More research is needed.

Single-parent home

Effects depend on the adjustment of the parent and available support systems outside the home. An intact family does not appear to be an important variable in predicting normal development.

Poverty

Effects vary depending on family adjustment and support. Availability of extrafamilial support also appears to be important. There is a somewhat higher rate of child abuse in poverty-level families.

SINGLE PARENTING AND DIVORCE

It is no secret that the incidence of divorce and single-parent households is increasing at an alarming rate. According to a recent survey published in the Los Angeles *Times*, the United States has the highest incidence of divorce and single-parent families in the world. (In 1986, births to unmarried women accounted for 23.4 percent of all live births.)

Single parents—whether divorced, widowed, or unmarried—must shoulder enormous emotional, psychological, and financial burdens. Unfortunately, in nearly every case, these stresses will affect children of all ages to some degree.

INFANTS AND DIVORCE

As Linda Francke states in *Growing Up Divorced* (Simon & Schuster, 1983), "(N)o child is too young to experience the fallout from divorce." For infants, most experts agree that the effects of a divorce are *indirect*. The early loss or absence of one parent (in most cases the father) can result in a number of potential problems.

Infants are aware of a *parent's* stress, not their own. Like the effects of second-hand smoke, the pain of divorce or the burdens of parenting alone may cloud an infant's world and keep him from receiving the ideal amounts of stimuli and attention he might otherwise receive.

As we have seen, stage-appropriate stimuli are vitally important for babies and toddlers. As the infant approaches six months of age, he has certainly learned to recognize differences in faces. His ability to distinguish people's faces visually is important; it marks a heightened interest in discovering the world by means of his five senses. If only one parent is available, active use of the senses decreases dramatically. Without the visual stimulation of two or three faces constantly around him, the baby doesn't have to work as hard.

What's more, a tense parent struggling alone to manage many tasks may not be able to respond fully and effectively to an infant's emotional needs. In turn, the infant my become unresponsive, and this cycle of sluggish response may become routine. Single parents are probably well advised to "draft" new faces; ask family, friends, or neighbors to pay the baby a visit and broaden exposure to new people.

If an infant has his basic needs met (feeding, changing, cuddling, stroking, etc.), a sense of trust will follow. The difficulty is this; even with two parents, there are moments of genuine fatigue, frustration, and short tempers associated with the daily demands of caring for an infant. Obviously, if a parent is dealing with the burdens of raising a child alone, there may be times when a changing or a feeding becomes a frustrating chore instead of an opportunity to communicate in a nurturing way.

But don't despair! Since every home situation is different, the consequences for individual infants will be different as well. Remember that the goal is to maximize stage-appropriate play. Though it will take work, single parents can and have managed this quite successfully.

Above all, separated parents should make a concerted effort to avoid a situation in which they "share" a baby younger than one year old. Moving the infant from one home to the other can be extremely disorienting and leave your child confused at a critical growth stage. The child should be kept in *either* home, in familiar surroundings, with at least one constant caregiver. Arrangements should be made for the parent to visit the child, instead of vice-versa. This type of arrangement establishes the consistency that a newborn must have in order to begin to feel genuinely secure. Such security, in turn, provides the foundation necessary for the infant to learn trust.

The question for single parents is often not *how* to introduce proper stimulation but *when* to do so. Days may speed past, leaving both parent and child feeling exhausted. You may feel that the many stresses and obligations you face leave no "slice" of you for the baby. In dealing with such obstacles, remember that your emotional state influences your child's in a profound way; try to approach the questions you face from a perspective of clearheadedness. Accentuating the negative or castigating yourself as a "bad parent" will only make the job you and your baby face more difficult.

Following are some ideas for getting the most out of your day with baby.

Share bath times. This may entail your swearing off showers for a while (most infants and toddlers don't like

them), but it can be well worth it. Reclaim the ten or fifteen minutes you normally rush through before baby
awakens—see what happens if you share the experience
of the warm, soapy water together.

*Make a point of playing games during changing and cleanup
periods.* Some parents play music to make a diaper
change go more smoothly. Others make a point of turning colored mobiles above the changing table.

Encourage non-television oriented play. There's certainly
nothing wrong with a good episode of *Sesame Street*, but
try to make sure your child is exposed to a number of
different play activities that can be undertaken "semi-in-
dependently." (This means you keep one eye on your
child as she plays in a safe area with a rattle or pull toy,
but still manage to finish some of the work you brought
home for the night.)

"OVERPARENTING"

"Overparenting" poses problems as the infant reaches about six months of age. At this point, a baby is beginning to experience independence—for example, crawling away from you, or trying to hold a bottle alone. If a parent "smothers" the baby by completing or preempting such attempts (perhaps overcompensating for time spent at the office and not at home), the baby might become irritable and frustrated.

Love and attention are essential, but unfortunately *too* much hugging and squeezing may lead to stalled growth patterns. Babies certainly need attention and stimulation, but they also need to manage challenges. (Like the rest of us, they need a break now and then as well.)

"UNDERPARENTING"

"Underparenting," too, can present problems. An example of this might be the parent who does not or cannot respond adequately to her baby's needs because she is trying to reestablish her life after being divorced, separated, or widowed. The parent's own emotional and psychological problems might temporarily overwhelm her and take away the strength she needs to foster a secure, nurturing relationship with the baby. These feelings might then cause a new mother to become frustrated and overly critical of herself. At the very least, the baby's physical needs should be tended to as quickly and as lovingly as possible; no matter what the mother's emotional state is, it is vital that someone be there for the child.

Most importantly, underparenting adversely affects the development of a routine of "play" times for the child. Play is a stimulating element of interaction that most experts feel is necessary for social and cognitive development. Some single mothers may need some help with fostering an atmosphere in which the child can interact with another person in a playful manner. This is a very workable—and sometimes essential—option.

TODDLERS AND DIVORCE

Children aged approximately 12 to 24 months experience divorce differently than infants. Francke observes that at this age, the impacts of divorce now become direct. The toddler who has bonded with both parents must somehow accept that one of those parents will no longer be a permanent part of his life. The familiarity, the consistency of routine that the parents worked together to establish for the child—this is now altered forever.

Separation anxiety can increase a toddler's fears of being abandoned, and this is not surprising. The toddler can only comprehend the divorce by applying what he already knows. For example, a toddler might be afraid of even a temporary separation from the remaining parent, reasoning that if Daddy decided to go away, Mommy might, too, if left to her own devices.

Many experts feel that at two years of age (but not before), a child should be able to spend alternate periods of time with each parent. Two-year-olds have begun to experience exciting feelings of independence from their parents; this is essential for their development. Their attempts to break free are tentative, however, and they need to feel that someone will be there for them at all times. Therefore, a consistent routine that incorporates both parents can be workable—and quite stimulating at that.

DAYCARE

In her *All Day Care* (Random House, 1990), Susan M. Zitman explains that the first year of life is the most important. With this in mind, new mothers may simply resign themselves to a year at home—and for these women, daycare is not an issue (at least for the time being). Staying home during this period can be very rewarding; it is universally accepted that, during the first year, an infant is changing and growing at a rate that is unparalleled in any other time frame of its life.

Those new mothers who must consider whether to place their infants in daycare centers face a battery of arguments for and against early daycare (that type of daycare provided for infants and toddlers younger than two years old). Most experts agree, however, that since infants younger than one year need an environment that features high levels of nurturing and enriching interactions, some types of day care are not in the best interest of these infants. It is also true, however, that group day care might benefit an older child aged between 13 and 24 months. The final decision must take into account the age and developmental patterns of the individual child.

Fredelle Bruser Maynard, in her book *The Child Care Crisis* (Simon & Schuster, 1985), presents reasons why mothers should think twice before placing an infant in daycare. The most important reason not to is that an infant recognizes his or her mother—and is well aware when that mother is absent.

We must remember that a baby knows his or her mother, not in an intellectual sense, but by scent, sound, and touch. Babies can tell the difference between a mother's touch and that of an unknown person. Experts agree that a baby needs, above all, such *familiar* caretaker signals consistently. Daycare situations in which the caregivers change randomly are doubtless bewildering to a three-month old child, and possibly quite terrifying. It is hard to imagine that insecurity would not be a prominent feature of the emotional makeup of a baby in such a setting.

There are more problems with multiple caretakers at daycare centers. Babies require an environment that is consistent with regard to affection and stimulation. If there are several rotating caretakers, each with a different overall approach, an infant probably will not get sufficient consistent intellectual stimulation, and this may affect development. Again, such a circumstance is not a disaster, and any effects are not irreversible, but new parents should certainly avoid a rotating-caretaker daycare situation if at all possible. Opt for one in which your child receives consistent care from one individual.

Placing an infant or toddler in a daycare setting does carry with it the risk of what Maynard calls "anxious avoidant attachments.'" Translated, this means that when the parent comes to the daycare facility to pick up his or her child, that child is more likely to respond unfavorable—and may avoid contact and resist affection. This interferes with the still-developing parent-child bond.

For older children in this group (those roughly 13 to 24 months old), separation anxiety can be a problem, even if the child and parents have developed strong attachments. Children at this age have just enough intelligence to understand that Mommy or Daddy are leaving, but not enough to understand that after a period of time they will be back. Time is a mystery to children at this age. Some will adapt to the separation better than others.

Watch your toddler's reactions—and try to develop a system that works for everyone.

APPENDIX D

What is Bonding?

W HAT EXACTLY DO WE MEAN when we say that a child has "bonded" with a parent?

Some experts make a distinction between "bonding" and "attachment," using "bonding" to describe the parents' developing feelings toward a child, and "attachment" to refer to the feelings an infant develops toward parents. The two terms are, nevertheless, used interchangeably by most lay people, and we can use the word "bonding" here to describe the overall process of initial emotional interconnection and commitment between very young children and their parents.

Bonding is undeniably important; some studies have even concluded that lack of sufficient bonding and emotional connection in infancy can lead to an inability to form close relationships later in life. This remains a very broad view of the issue, however. The most important question is not whether or not bonding with parents is advisable—it is in fact an essential component of infant development—but how to ensure that bonding takes place in an enriching framework.

We must remember that sensory development is an infant's first link to the outside world—and is an essential part of the child's very earliest human relationships, as well. Sensory development plays an important role in the establishment of an infant's trust, in large measure because it is such a key consideration in helping to alert caretakers to daily needs like feeding and changing (through the infant's act of crying). Once a baby's needs are met, the very first feelings of trust can take root. This is an indispensable part of the bonding process.

Physical contact—whether it takes the form of soothing strokes or gentle patting motions—bring an infant feelings of pleasure and a sense of calm. Dr. T.B. Brazelton's research on the bonding process indicates that an infant's sense of touch is vital because it is the primary means of communication. Watch a newborn being held or nursed, and you will be witnessing, in that intrinsically physical contact, the primordial means of human intimate interaction.

MEASURING THE EFFECTS OF PHYSICAL CONTACT

How do we know that early physical contact is so vitally important? In a 1990 study at the Columbia University College of Physicians and Surgeons, Elizabeth Anisfield and a group of colleagues measured the effects of the degree of physical contact on the development of infant-mother attachment. The results were intriguing.

In these experiments, the degree of contact was controlled by placing the mother/infant pairs into two groups. One group was given soft baby carriers known by the commercial name "Snugli." The Snugli is a pouch-type carrier similar to carriers used in parts of Africa that supports the infant so that she rests securely on the mother's chest. The pouch has the additional advantage of leaving the mother's hands fee, so the infant can accompany her as she carries out her daily activities. This chest-to-chest contact provided the babies of this first group with warmth, comfort, human contact, and nurturing.

The second group of mothers was given plastic carriers (similar to car-seats) that featured a large handle for transport. This type of carrier—which researchers have thought not to promote emotional interconnection between mothers and infants—allows the mother to transport her baby with little or no physical contact necessary.

The establishment of these two groups was made very early in the developmental process—shortly after the mothers gave birth. The group given Snuglis was designated as the experimental group, and those given plastic infant seats were designated as the control group.

After thirteen months, the infants in the experimental group were found to have formed a closer attachment to their mothers, as measured through clinical observation. In addition, the experimental mothers proved to be more responsive to their children!

Such results support Dr. Brazelton's view that touch is essential for promoting the bonding process.

DEGREES OF ATTACHMENT

Anisfield's experiment also measured some interesting indicators of the degree of attachment during the thirteen months.

For example, at three and a half months, the mother/infant pairs were assessed against two criteria: looking behavior and vocalization of the babies. To measure the looking behavior, the mothers were asked to play with the infant on a mattress on the floor, with the infant propped up on a cushion in order to face the mother. A mirror was placed behind the infant's head, enabling researchers to take advantage of a clearer view of the faces of both mother and infant. The experiment required mothers to play with their babies for fifteen minutes without using any toys; the entire process was videotaped.

Upon the completion of these sessions, the tapes were meticulously analyzed. Of greatest interest to researchers was the number of times mother and baby established eye contact; this factor was monitored and the number of eye-meetings recorded.

The results were conclusive: those babies who had been carried in the Snuglis spent significantly more time looking at their mothers' faces than the babies who had been carried in plastic seats. However, it is interesting to note that, because the development we are reviewing runs along two tracks, involving both mother and child (and not child alone), the *mother's* responsiveness is just as important as the baby's. Anisfield is careful to note that the disparity in eye-contact between the two groups "could be related to the fact that (the) mothers (in the control group) were generally less responsive."

The conclusion for parents from this part of the experiment, then, may be that it is not just "good for your baby" to provide lots of close physical contact during infancy, but good *for the relationship you establish with the baby* to do so!

As we noted, the Anisfield study also measured the infants' levels of vocalization. The results indicated that the control infants—those carried in the plastic seats—were more inclined to vocalize alone. This finding supported the theory that infants use vocalization to achieve proximity and closeness; if the infants are not physically close to the mother (as the babies in the Snuglis often were), they will attempt to achieve that closeness by vocalizing alone to get the mother's attention.

This view that infants come into the world readily equipped with a system of behavior that they use to achieve closeness with their caregivers (for example, smiling or crying) has been around for some time. According to this theory, attachment is promoted as the infant's attempts to achieve closeness are consistently successful (for example, through a parent answering a baby's cry, or returning a happy expression when a baby begins to smile).

Recent studies take theories of attachment one step further, and suggest that what matters is not just whether an infant's calls for attention are answered, but *how* they are answered. A 1985 survey by Main, Kaplan, and Cassidy suggests that the manner in which adults respond has a huge impact on the nature of the bonding relationship. Many experts feel, for example, that an infant whose mother responds to his cries with soft, loving words and caresses will establish a stronger and more trusting relationship than the mother who reacts in a distracted, uneasy, or rushed way.

CAN INFANTS BOND WITH MORE THAN ONE PERSON?

Some new parents may be curious to learn the extent to which their baby can bond with non-parents. Experts agree that babies can and do bond with several people, including those who may not be family members, but this is really no cause for alarm. The fact that a baby can bond with others cannot make *your* bonding experience with your child any less significant.

In a recent article in *Parents* magazine, Dr. Katherine Karlsrud, a clinical instructor of pediatrics at Cornell University Medical College, cites feelings of safety and trust as the prerequisites to the bonding process. Once these feelings have been established, Karlsrud notes, the infant feels secure, and in a secure environment where an infant has emotional responses from those around him, bonding can occur with any person with whom the baby interacts on a regular basis, including relatives and babysitters.

The bonding process requires true caring, not just the mechanical fulfillment of the baby's physical needs. Dr. Karlsrud emphasizes that attending to daily feedings or changes with a brash, perfunctory air simply ignores the baby's emotional needs; in order to make the person-to-person contact essential for a sense of security and later self-development, the order of the day is genuine interest, eye contact, smiling, and lots of gentle touching.

First Born,
Second Born

Is IT EASIER FOR PARENTS WHEN THEY only have one child? In the usual situation, a home with only one child is one which is more peaceful and less problematic than one with multiple siblings. In this type of home, the child interacts mainly with the parents. On occasion, the child gets to play with another young child such as a neighbor or a family member, but the parents generally remain the key agents of social interaction.

Most babies in this situation are well taken care of. Parents of an only child generally have more time to devote to their newborn. The novelty and excitement of a newborn, especially the first one, is so compelling that the baby stands to gain all the attention he needs.

The benefits of the undivided attention that a first-born baby receives may be obvious; what is not so obvious is that this benefit translates into long term positive effects as well. For example, research has shown that first born children turn out to be professionally more successful than younger siblings. This outcome is attributable to the steady, supportive environment that is provided by parents.

In contrast, younger siblings tend to be more disruptive, more innovative, freer and more spontaneous. This too makes sense psychologically, since the younger sib-

lings tend to interact not only with parents but with older
siblings. They learn to cope with their sometimes challenging multi-sibling environment and be more inventive.

SIBLING RIVALRY

Are jealousy, rivalry, and hostility between young children natural? Yes. These situations aren't irregular or abnormal at all. Expect them.

Many child psychologists believe that sibling rivalry
stems from the older child's feelings of loss, of not being
loved as much as before. When a younger sibling enters
the scene and takes away some of the attention and love
that was previously the older child's exclusive property,
a certain feeling of loss is inevitable.

One obvious manifestation of this is aggressive behavior of the older child toward the newborn baby. Aggressive behavior can range from taking things that belong
to the baby to physically hurting him. Sometimes, in an
attempt to recapture the exclusive attention that once be-
longed to him, the toddler tries to become a baby again.
In this case, he regresses to more infantile modes of actions, such as speech patterns, toilet training, and eating
and sleeping problems.

All of these occasionally alarming actions are part of a
plan to "get even" with the younger baby. The older child
invariably feels that the newborn has penetrated his do-
main, and has taken the exclusive right to receiving his
parents' attention. Now that attention must be shared
with someone else. Getting even is a natural reaction to
someone taking something away—in this case, parental
attention.

One way to avoid or minimize these problems is to
"space" children two to three years apart. An older child,
for example a three-year-old, is better able to cope with a

newcomer than a one-year-old because his social life no longer revolves solely around his parents or his immediate home environment. A three-year-old usually has the company of one or more playmates at least part of the time.

Spacing children too closely to one another, less than three years apart, is challenging for both the children and parents.

By the age of 8 to 12 months, a baby learns to cope with the aggressive behavior of an older sibling—in other words, he is able to defend himself and retaliate. And all parents can attest to the "negative phase" which children go through in Stages 5 and 6. This stage of resisting help from parents, testing wills, and constantly saying "no" can sometimes be redirected toward the older sibling when the children are spaced too closely together.

What if you are faced with the question of how best to handle the conflicts that arise when children are born within twenty-four months of each other? Here are some suggestions.

• Maintain an off-limits play area for the baby.

• Keep the toys of the older sibling separate from those of the baby. This will minimize "ownership challenges."

• Encourage the older sibling to express his or her emotions about the new situation through healthy outlets. Such outlets would include knocking over blocks, hitting punching bags, or kicking play balls outdoors.

• Explain in a clear, non-threatening way that it is all right to be angry or hurt.

• Treat every vocal expression of pain or rage as a positive. Be patient. It is better for your child to say the things he or she feels than to suppress them.

• Even though your own resilience and energy level will be low, try to make a point of noticing and applauding those areas where the older sibling excels in ways the baby cannot. Regular applications of genuine positive attention along these lines will soothe bruised toddler egos.

Finally, remember that this stage will not last forever. With tolerance, love, and mutual support, your family will emerge stronger for the experience.

◆

Recommended Commercially Available Toys

◆

THE FOLLOWING TOYS, PRESENTED IN ORDER of manufacturer/brand name, have high play value and durability and are suitable for enriching developmental play. Where appropriate, age guidelines are given.

Baby Tomy

Push-go-round
(birth to eighteen months)

Disney

Activity gym

Musical mobiles

Pluto rocker

Ride-on Mickey

Soft crib pals

Wrist rattles

Educaring

Puzzle cubes
(colorful interlocking pieces; eighteen months and older)

The First Year

First keys
(numbered; one month to three years)

First rattle
(like phone handle; birth to eighteen months)

Soft teething beads
(three months and older)

Fisher-Price

Activity blocks
(crib and playpen toy; blocks can be stacked, nested, toted; each block has different activity; six to thirty months)

Activity center
(dial; mirror; roll drum; push-squeaker bunny; knob that turns picture wheel; sliding animals; pushbutton rings bell; bright ball rotates; knob jiggles sun picture; color spinning wheel; three to eighteen months)

Activity pots and pans
(can be stacked; tom-tom drum with see-through bottom, whistle spoon, squeaker lid handle, etc.; three pans and one lid; six to thirty months)

Activity train stroller toy
(train attached to stroller; six to twenty-four months)

Animal grabbers: Rosie Rabbit, Billy Bear, Ellery Elephant
(each with different texture, sounds; eyes sewn tightly; machine-washable, dryer-safe; birth to two years)

Animal sounds barn
(five different sounds; levers and buttons produce movement; nine to thirty-six months)

Baby's first blocks
(twelve sturdy plastic blocks in shape-sorter canister; six to twenty-four months)

Bathtub duck
(floating Puffalump duck in innertube; six to twenty-four months)

Fisher-Price (continued)

Chime ball
(roly-poly chime toy that floats; three to thirty-six months)

Crib wraparound
(clicking peek-a-boo train door)

Crib wraparound
(shatterproof mirror turtle)

Crib wraparound
(squeaking woolly lamb)

Crib wraparound
(tug-a-lug Humpty Dumpty)

Dancing animals music box mobile
(ten-minute wind-up music box; animals angled to face baby; birth to six months)

Discovery bunny
(various rattle sounds, chewable carrot teething ring, tug-gable tail, mirror in tummy, paw in squeaker, etc.; three to twenty-four months)

Discovery schoolhouse and cottage
(little people, bells, buttons, sliding panels; twelve to thirty-six months)

Farm sound friends
(movement produces various barnyard animal sounds; three to thirty months)

Floating fun
(suction base holds whale, turtle, bird in place for bath-time play; six to twenty-four months)

Lights and sounds piano
(requires batteries; three musical keys light up with baby's touch; roll drum to play three songs; six to thirty-six months)

Musical activity center
(sliding objects make noise; clicking dial; sliding puppy activates music box and rotating picture wheel; three to eighteen months)

Fisher-Price (continued)

Musical hug-n-tug bird
(tug on tail makes bird "dance"; built-in rattle and squeaker; music-box tune; birth to twenty-four months)

Pick up and go dump truck
(block-gobbling walker converts to activity truck; shape sorter built into cab; colorful blocks for loading; nine to thirty-six months)

Play gym
(suspended from plastic rod; roller beads in transparent bubble, spinning shapes; birth to five months)

Poppity-pop car
(beads pop when car is rolled; six to twenty-four months)

Pop-up bunny
(rolling drum makes bunny pop up; six to thirty months)

Puffalump series
(soft animals, some with built-in rattle; birth to twenty-four months)

Red ring rocker
(bright red teething ring with a free-spinning horse in center that turns, makes "clip-clop" sound; three to eighteen months)

Rocking pony
("clip-clops" when rocked; soft padded mane; twelve to thirty months)

Shiny shaker
(tubular rattle with brightly colored teething rings; sparkles; three to eighteen months)

Smile and play mirror
(for crib or floor; built-in stand; sliding rings; birth to thirty months)

Snack and play tray
(activity center featuring squeakers and spinners)

Snap-lock beads
(fit together to form chain; various colors; six to thirty-six months)

Fisher-Price *(continued)*

Soft sounds cassette/tape player mobile
(mobile with picture disk; various sounds keyed to developmental levels of babies zero to six months, six to eighteen months, and eighteen to thirty-six months)

Store and stack mailbox
(fill-and-spill, sort-and-stack mailbox with five colorful "postcards"; nine to thirty-six months)

Stroller toy
(six activities; attaches to stroller)

Teether/rattle combination
(apple with rocking horse; birth to eighteen months)

Teether/rattle combination
(bunny with strawberry shape; birth to eighteen months)

Teether/rattle combination
(ring with colorful beads; birth to eighteen months)

Toddler kitchen
(ten activities; twelve to thirty-six months)

Turn and learn activity center
(with peek-a-boo mirror, sliding ABCs, springy 1-2-3 bear, and clicking shape/color dial; six to twenty-four months)

Wrist rattle with velcro attachment
(machine-washable, dryer-safe; panda face; bright red with white dots; birth to twelve months)

Xylo-drum
(one side is a three-key xylophone, the other a drum; six to thirty-six months)

Johnson & Johnson

Crib activity arch
(toys alone, birth to twelve months; arch, birth to five months)

Rings and rollers
(six to twenty-four months)

Johnson & Johnson *(continued)*

Wiggle worm
   (birth to twelve months)

Yo-yo rattle
   (birth to eighteen months)

Gerry Early Images

Video picture book
   (VHS; enhances sight/sound discovery; birth to twelve
   months)

Lego

Preschool sets
   (big interconnecting blocks; many play sets; eighteen
   months to five years)

Muppet Babies

Activity blanket

Inflatable rollaround
   (transparent, weighted with ball)

Mirror

Pop-up activity lever toys

Pansy Allen

Smart Starts musical mobile
   (all black-and-white, with rings, mirror, animals)

Playskool

Baby's first books
   (part of "Touch 'Ems" series; fabric; nine soft textures; lift-
   and-look activities; six to twenty-four months)

Busy bath
   (seven-activity center for the tub; eighteen to thirty-six
   months)

Playskool (continued)

Busy beads
(beads run along twisted wire paths; mounted on small platform; eighteen months to five years)

Busy Big Bird
(five activities; six to twenty-four months)

Busy camera
(six to twenty-four months)

Busy choo-choo
(six to twenty-four months)

Busy elephant
(seven activities; six to twenty-four months)

Busy fire truck
(six to twenty-four months)

Busy guitar
(six to twenty-four months)

Busy popper plane
(six activities including push-and-pull pop balls; six to twenty-four months)

Busy pounding bench
(reversible bench with three attached colorful pegs; easy-to-hold mallet to squeak and pound; twelve to twenty-four months)

Busy soft wheels
(fabric cars with six activities; six to eighteen months)

Busy workshop
(drop chute; lift-out bucket; sliding saw; sliding "storage" doors; big nuts and bolts for sorting and stacking; nails with "boing" sound; rattle hammer; ratcheting vise with rotating handles; pretend paintbrush; nine to twenty-four months)

Kiddie links
(14 colorful links; teethable; sorting, many combinations; six to thirty-six months)

Playskool *(continued)*

Busy car
(large blue ride-in car; busy dashboard with squeak and click activities; door opens; nine to thirty months)

Busy pop-up phone
(roll drum, blue phone, yellow buttons, picture lever; six to twenty-four months)

Clutch ball
(part of "Touch 'Ems" series; soft, colorful ball with six different textures; three to eighteen months)

Color and contrast busy box
(ten sight, sound, and touch activities)

Color and contrast kitty
(rattle; teethable rings)

Color and contrast musical busy box
(sixteen activities)

Color and contrast peek-a-boo books
(three peek-and-play activities; two happy sounds; three special textures; soft, bold, bright colors stimulate visual activity; six to twenty-four months)

Color and contrast puppy
(rattle; teethable rings)

Color and contrast soft rattles
(various types)

Color and contrast teether rattles
(various types)

Dapper Dan
(dressing doll with button, snap, zip, bow-tie, buckle; twelve months to five years)

Plastic keys
(large, attachable keys; primary colors; three to eighteen months)

Fold and go quilt
(folds into tote; ten activities; birth to eighteen months)

Playskool *(continued)*

Foot jingles
(Sesame Street footies that rattle; birth to six months)

Pull-along truck
(carries wooden blocks; eighteen months to five years)

Rattles
(wide variety; many with Sesame Street and Disney characters)

Sounds around
(put dial on picture, pull cord to hear sound; eighteen months and older)

Squeezables
(Muppets and others; soft; not cloth)

Steady steps little walker
(looks like shopping cart; nine to twenty-four months)

Steady steps walker/doll stroller
(with spinning beads; nine to thirty-six months)

Wee wheels
("baby's first vehicle"; easy-hold handle; rattle sound; simple and small; three to twenty-four months)

Weebles activity copter
(eight activities; eight to thirty-six months)

Weebles farm
(with tractor and three shape-sortable animals; eight to thirty-six months)

Weebles gas station
(with little car; ten sounds and activities; eight to thirty-six months)

Weebles vehicles
(large Weebles; eight to thirty-six months)

Sesame Street

Big Bird roll-back toy
(roll it away, it rolls back; one to five years)

Sesame Street (continued)

Carseat toy

Crib/playpen toy

Roly-poly toys

Stroller toy

Shellykins

Musical baby ball
(air-filled chime ball, makes sounds at baby's touch; three to twenty-four months)

Shelcore

Build-a-ball toy
(plastic pieces fit together; primary colors)

◆

GLOSSARY

accommodation

The process of changing oneself in response to the demands imposed by a present situation. Whenever a baby changes a present scheme of doing things because the situation demands such a change, he is accommodating.

assimilation

The process by which the baby relates a new object, feeling, or act to what is already known. This process is automatically applied to new encounters. When new encounters don't fit into prior knowledge, accommodation may result.

concrete operational stage

The third phase in intellectual development, which appears at approximately seven years of age and lasts through about age twelve. In this stage, the child can use logical operations involving concrete events, but not abstract ones.

coordination

The process through which the baby unites actions together to form more complicated actions. It is through coordination that a baby expands his activity. Actions are the origins of knowledge, whereas coordinations constitute the means by which knowledge multiplies.

development

The general process of intellectual and physical growth, which comes about through the interaction of maturation, physical experience, social transmission, and equilibration.

empirical abstraction

The process of constructing knowledge of the physical properties of the world. In infancy, this results in a rudimentary understanding of the physical properties of objects and their broadly understood interactions with one another.

equilibration

An ongoing process of balancing what is known with the to-be-known. This is a self-regulating motivational process inherent to knowing. Its task is to constantly monitor new experiences and try to make sense of them in terms of what is already known.

formal operational stage

The fourth and final phase of intellectual development, appearing at approximately twelve to fourteen years of age in children in urbanized communities. This phase is characterized by the ability to use logic not only concretely, but in an abstract way as well. Hypothetical deductive logic is among the hallmarks of this stage.

learning

The process of integrating specific information into one's prior knowledge.

logico-mathematical knowledge

Knowledge derived from acting on one's actions; a know-how of one's actions. This form of knowledge is the basis of inferential thought.

operation

An organized action that is internalized and that can be mentally reversed. An operation implies a logical structure because it can be reversed.

physical knowledge

Knowledge of the physical properties of the empirical world. This is constructed from direct interactions with objects and events.

preoperational stage

The period of intellectual development spanning (approximately) the years two through seven. This period is characterized by the inability to utilize logical operations. The preoperational child is unable to reverse mental actions (operations).

primary circular reaction

The baby's repetition of a bodily action that produces an interesting effect obtained by chance.

reflective abstraction

The process through which one derives logico-mathematical knowledge. This process is reflective in that one derives a know-how of one's abilities to manipulate one's own actions.

reversibility

The aspect of a logical operation that enables it to retrace its path. Logical reversibility does not manifest itself until about age seven, when the child can take some logical steps and mentally return to the beginning-point.

scheme

A plan of action that can be generalized to similar objects and events. When a baby sucks his thumb and then generalizes the action to his rattle or his feet, he is exercising a scheme of sucking.

secondary circular reaction

The phenomenon in which a baby's actions inadvertently produce an interesting result in his environment—an action that is repeated in order to reproduce the result.

sensori-motor stage

The period in intellectual development spanning birth through the first two years. It is characterized by a pre-lingual form of intelligence that is fundamentally action oriented.

symbolic function

A system for mentally representing actions and events, including language, mental images, imitation, symbolic play, and abbreviated gestures.

tertiary circular reactions

The phenomenon similar to a secondary circular reaction with the exception that the baby is no longer satisfied with merely reproducing the outcome, but invents new actions to discover their effects.

BIBLIOGRAPHY

Braga, Joseph D. and Laurie L.
Child Development and Early Childhood Education.
Chicago: Model Cities-Chicago Committee on Urban
Opportunity, 1973.

Cataldo, Christine
Infant and Toddler Programs: A Guide to Very Early Education.
Reading, Massachusetts: Addison-Wesley, 1983.

Einon, Dorothy
Play With a Purpose.
New York: Pantheon Books, 1986.

Francke, Linda
Growing Up Divorced.
New York: Simon & Schuster, 1983.

Gordon, Ira
*Baby Learning Through Baby Play: A Parent's Guide for the First
Two Years of Life.*
New York: St. Martin's Press, 1970.

Grasselli, Rose N. and Hegner, Priscilla A.
*Playful Parenting: Games to Help Your Infants and Toddlers
Grow Physically, Mentally, and Emotionally.*
New York: Richard Marek Publishers, 1981.

Jacob, S.H.
Foundations for Piagetan Education.
Lanham, Maryland: University Press of America, 1984.

Lehane, Stephen
Help Your Baby Learn: 100 Piaget-Based Activities for the First Two Years of Life.
Englewood Cliffs, New Jersey: Prentice-Hall, 1976.

McCall, Robert B.
Infants.
Cambridge: Harvard University Press, 1979.

Liebert, Robert M., Wicks-Nelson, Rita, and Kail, Robert.
Developmental Psychology.
Englewood Cliffs, New Jersey: Prentice-Hall, 1984.

Maynard, Fredelle Bruser
The Child Care Crisis.
New York: Simon & Schuster, 1985.

Newson, John and Elizabeth
Toys and Playthings.
London: George Allen & Unwin, 1979.

Piaget, Jean
The Origins of Intelligence in Children.
New York: International Universities Press, 1952

Restak, Richard M.
The Brain: The Last Frontier.
New York: Warner Books, 1979.

Smolak, Linda
Infancy.
Englewood Cliffs, New Jersey: Prentice-Hall, 1986

Sroufe, L. Alan
Child Development: Its Nature and Course
New York: Alfred A. Knopf, 1988

Saunders, Ruth, and Bingham-Newman, Ann M.
Piagetan Perspective for Preschools: A Thinking Book for Teachers.
Englewood Cliffs, New Jersey: Prentice-Hall, 1984.

Smolak, Linda
Infancy.
Englewood Cliffs, New Jersey: Prentice-Hall, 1986.

Zitman, Susan
All Day Care.
New York: Random House, 1990.

INDEX